THINGS
I WISH
I KNEW

A Compendium of Lessons Learned Late

FRED WITT

To my three gifts, Aaron, Tyler and Olivia.

You inspire me.

CONTENTS

CONTENTS

CONTENTS

would answer my friend's questions about life and how to live it. I was a Midwestern boy with Midwestern values and my method for handling problems was to use a simple, common sense approach. I was always viewed as reasonable. Aren't all guys named "Fred" reasonable by definition? With each year and every answer, I grew in my perspective and understanding of human nature. And I learned even more about myself, as a more perfectly imperfect human being. It was like slowly peeling an onion.

At the end of these conversations, even with strangers, they would say, "I've never heard it put that way. Why don't you write a book?" Well ... their collective voices stuck in my mind and ... here it is. Here are the things I wish I knew. The lessons I learned late. I hope there is something in these pages you find valuable and learn early. Some words of wisdom you can apply to make your life a little easier. Or maybe just a new perspective – "Oh, now I get it!"

This book is based on my experience, not my research. I'm no expert, that's for sure. In fact, there's probably not much written that you didn't already know or haven't previously read in some self-help book written by an "expert." But I haven't found a book written by a kind-hearted friend from the Midwest who brings a lawyer's perspective to bear. When times get tough, he's the guy you call. You do so because you know he understands what you are going through – he can empathize. He's not judgmental because he's either been through it or seen it at work. And when the conversation's over, you know you'll feel a little better. It's often a relief just to realize you're not the first person in the history of mankind with this problem.

I've tried to provide my thoughts in a way that's clear and actionable. Basically, if you had me as a friend, and you could ask me a life/relationship/child-rearing question, what would I tell you? Sometimes I'd give you advice. Sometimes I'd tell you a story. But as a friend, I'd tell you what you need to hear, not what you want to hear. And you'd listen and process. Sometimes you'd take the advice, sometimes you'd ignore it. Often you'd take "bits and pieces" and adapt them to your way of doing things. There's no magic. Its just life, lived one day at a time with each of us doing our best.

Put a little differently, I wish someone had read the current literature, conducted the research, and then condensed it down to simple thoughts with concrete action steps. Things that made sense and things I could remember in my time of need. Then I wish a good friend had seen me making a mess of my life (at the moment), bought the book and hit me over the head with it. There's no question I've always needed some sense knocked into me. Then, in their kindest, most sympathetic voice, my friend would've barked: "Here, knucklehead, read this before you prove all your critics right!"

This book is organized in the way adult life unfolds. You try to find a great job. You search for that special someone. You have kids and discover they don't come with an instruction booklet either. A note of caution: our ride together may get bumpy, so you'd better buckle up!

PART I: CAREER COUNSELING

1. FOUR WORDS FOR SUCCESS

Over the years, I've thought deeply about what makes a person successful. It's not difficult to come up with a list of ten things a person needs to do to succeed. But who can remember ten things, much less take action on them all? To be actionable, the concepts must be simple and easy to remember. I've wondered if I could reduce the list to not just three or four phrases or concepts, but three or four words. Words that represent core principles upon which other ideals are built.

With that challenge in mind, here is my list of four words, which, if lived by, I'm convinced will lead to a life of success:

•**Goal**. Set a new goal each day and work diligently to achieve it. It should be a tiny goal. One that can be achieved within that day. The goal could be to study an extra 15 minutes, treat everyone you meet today with greater respect, eat a healthy lunch (maybe substitute fruit for French fries) or take the stairs instead of the elevator. A "goal a day" is profound because it's easy to add to your daily routine. It's understandable. It's achievable. Can you imagine how much better you'd be if you achieved a new goal every day of your life?

•**Laugh**. Laugh not only with others, but especially laugh at life and the things that happen to you. We can't control what happens to us, only how we react. Make it a priority to laugh with your loved ones, especially your children. Imagine the kind of person you'd be if your heart was filled with the spirit of laughter. What if your first reaction was to laugh?

•**Love.** Do you know whom you should love? Yourself. Because you can't love others until and unless you love yourself first. What does your little voice say? Does it speak words of love to you? Not for most of us. In fact, just the opposite. We are our own worst critics. Imagine if you changed your inner voice and loved yourself first. Do you have compassion for yourself? You'll achieve "self love" when your little voice speaks positive words of compassion and support.

•**Accountability**. Be accountable to yourself and everyone around you, most especially your family and friends. Be accountable for your words, actions and deeds. This one is handy because we all know when we are and when we aren't being accountable. Do you know someone who's fully accountable? Imagine the kind of person you'd be if you lived a life of accountability.

LESSONS LEARNED LATE:

- Life is lived just one day at a time.
- Today is a gift. When will you unwrap it?
- To insure success, live your life based on four words:
    o   Goal
    o   Laugh
    o   Love
    o   Accountability
- If it helps, remember the acronym: GoaLLA
- Live without barriers.
- When you wake up tomorrow, imagine a fabulous, authentic life.
- Inspire others.
- Imagine this is your fortune: You have not yet lived the best days of your life.

2. FINDING A GREAT JOB

A. The Secret Sauce

You will spend most of your life "on the job." The time with co-workers, some known, many faceless, will dwarf that shared with your precious loved ones. Big decisions in life have big consequences. Have you carefully analyzed your hopes and dreams, strengths and weaknesses, talents and skills – and matched them with a career that's perfect for you? Do you have a great job? If not, what will it take to find one? What are you waiting for?

My first and most profound exposure to the subject of careers came from my Dad. He was a jeweler. He hammered, carved and bent bars of gold into beautiful rings. He did this for fifty years until the day he died at age eighty-one during his morning workout on a treadmill. He didn't make it that day, but he was still trying to get to work, just as he had his entire life. During his later years, friends and customers alike would ask the same question: "When you gonna retire, Fred?" He would answer "And do what?" The truth was, his most creative and profitable years designing and making jewelry happened after the age of sixty-five. Turns out, when others were retiring to their proverbial rocking chairs, Dad was setting sail on a new journey – a journey filled with his best work.

What I didn't understand about my Dad was that he had a secret. A secret that remained hidden from me for most of my life. (Education is so often lost on youth). I would always see him at work, in the store bearing his name. He would be sitting at a jeweler's workbench with a torch perpetually lit. The fire was burning, literally, but it looked tedious and uninteresting to me. I was always too busy running off somewhere to give much thought to why Dad always seemed so happy. And when I finally figured it out, it was almost too late.

Dad would laugh about being in the store six days a week and say to no one in particular: "Love what you do and you'll never work a day in your life." His secret was – to him, making jewelry wasn't a job. It was a hobby he was passionate about. Making jewelry was therapy for his soul. He got to work with his hands and his mind and allow his creative juices to flow. Then he also got the personal satisfaction of showing the beautiful wedding ring he'd designed and molded with his own hands to a newly engaged couple whose delight and wonder was contagious. He got to share in their soon to be wedded bliss knowing he'd had at least a small part in it. And he repeated this day after day for fifty years.

His secret was shockingly simple – find something you love and then pursue it with all your passion. If you're lucky enough to match your love with your skills, if you spend your daylight hours engaged in your hobby, "You'll never work a day in your life."

I'm often asked why I didn't go into business with Dad. There were many reasons, when only one would suffice: I had no artistic/creative ability. I could not have made a ring to save my soul. Dad was a brilliant, impatient, perfectionist and those characteristics all conspired to make him a lousy teacher. My going to work for him had "failure" written all over it and miraculously, we both knew it. I often joked about how lucky he was that I chose not to follow in his footsteps, because he would have had better luck trying to train a monkey!

LESSONS LEARNED LATE:

- Carefully think through what you're good at (and what you're not).
- Identify your passions (a hobby, perhaps?).
- List your job "must haves" and "deal breakers."
- Identify the lifestyles you'll be satisfied with and the trade-offs you're prepared to make (a forest ranger has the most beautiful "office" but is limited on pay).

- If you can't find it, create it (Dad started a jewelry business with a pair of pliers).

- Repeat after my Dad: "Love what you do and you'll never work a day in your life."

B. The Long Pursuit: A Study in Passion and Persistence

This is hardly a "news flash," but finding a great job takes time and effort. Rarely, does it show up "unannounced" in a basket on your doorstep. Most often, you have to overcome a lot of adversity and be prepared for a lot of rejection before you land that dream job. Maybe we're more aware of this than we think and it's part of the inertia that keeps us locked in our old one.

I've heard of some highly motivated folks who kept their first or most memorable rejection letter in their desk drawer. They did so because rejection can prove to be a supreme motivator. If you have any doubt, just tell a four-year-old they "can't" have something and watch their unbridled determination to get it. Entrepreneurs will tell you they never could find a job – they created it!

Since making jewelry was out, I had slightly narrowed the field of possibilities. But how do you even start the process? How do you know what your job skills are – what you're good at? As it turned out, the Chinese proverb ... "a journey of a thousand miles begins with a single step" seemed a perfect metaphor for my experience. My job search took forever and was littered with more rejection letters than I could count.

I attended a small, liberal arts college in the Midwest. As you might expect, it had robust English, Philosophy and Political Science departments, but only a small business program. I picked my classes based solely on the teacher – if I liked him/her, I ended up spending lots of hours in their department. I loved the spirit of one accounting professor (he would ride me endlessly in our classes of twelve students) and took every course he offered. He had many quirks.

quick because she knew we only had about fifteen minutes to eat. To this day, the meals at the Burr café were the best I've ever had. The green beans were fresh from the garden out back and the corn, well, you can only imagine how good it tasted.

My boss liked me, but, at the time, I didn't know what that meant. There were no performance evaluations. You either worked or got fired, whereupon you'd walk off the site into your old, dusty car and drive off, never to be part of the crew again. There were rules. Safety was first, because your life literally depended on it. You never drank on the job and if you showed up with a hint of alcohol on your breath, you were sent home without pay. Hangovers were allowed, of course, but the boss would sense weakness and he'd take special pleasure in making your life miserable that day. When we went out to a bar on Fridays, we could never start a fight. But we had to finish one provided we paid the bar owner for anything we broke. After all, we had a reputation to uphold.

Being liked had some positive benefits. The boss would yell "Freddy" and I'd hop up out of the hole. "Yes, boss, what do you want?" "I need you to get in the flatbed truck and get the supplies I've listed. They're waitin for ya, so get goin." Driving the truck was special because those were hours spent away from the shovel. Unlike many before me, I did what he asked and drove in a straight line, without detours to run personal errands or goof off. The boss never gave you words of approval. If he approved, he gave you something "good" to do twice in a row. Only later would I figure this out and understand the wisdom of his "people skills" and ability to motivate others (yes, fear worked well and was always a convenient starting place).

To my surprise, I discovered being liked had some negative consequences as well. Periodically, he would make an example out of me (sometimes just to deliver a message for my benefit, but more often for the crew's). Sometimes he would scream only at me when it had been the entire crew who'd messed up. He would give me some of the worst jobs too. Once, for an entire week, I had to crawl into the drum of a cement mixer and clean it out. The old cement dried on the steel flanges and I had to use a jackhammer to chip it off. Imagine the reverberations of a jackhammer inside a steel drum. I had a headache for weeks. And when I was 20 minutes late for work one day, he made a big "production" of it in front of the crew. Worse, he sent me home without pay. I was outraged and ready to quit. Another lesson learned late.

The combination of college and construction led me to the fall of my senior year. It was time to find a "real" job. Shoes polished (Dad told me "You can tell a man by his shoes"), I interviewed with two accounting firms on campus. I thought I did well – but I didn't even merit a rejection letter. It took me a little while to figure out I didn't get the job when I wasn't invited downtown for a second interview. So much for the value of polished shoes!

Now, what? I was graduating from college and had nothing to show for it. Dad was always telling me to get a skill – make sure you have something "they can never take away from you," he said. Being raised in the Depression, Dad learned that lesson the hard way. So, armed with his advice (and with nothing else in the hopper), I decided I'd go to law school. From my track record, you can probably imagine how this would go. Yup, you guessed it. I was approaching my senior year in law school and it was time to find a job with a law firm.

I interviewed with over thirty firms in Omaha, Kansas City, Denver, Portland and Seattle. Some quickly rejected me. From the others, I received two messages: (1) if you want to be a business tax lawyer, we only hire from the graduate tax program at New York University, or (2) it's come down to a decision between you and one other person. We'll get back to you. And, you guessed it, seemingly against the fifty/fifty odds, the "other" person always managed to get the job. I saved those rejection letters for many years.

After seven years of school and two degrees, I still had nothing to show for it. No job. No paycheck. No career. But I couldn't give up on my dream – my aspiration. Instead of giving up (or giving in), I did something else – I listened to "why" those firms rejected me. Turns out, their rejection offered a glimmer of hope – get an advanced law degree at the NYU graduate tax program – and come back and see us.

I took their advice. Why not? After all, I was running out of time and it was my last best hope. So, I gathered my savings (the construction job paid big bucks!), sold my car, and moved from Nebraska to New York City to attend NYU. Suffice it to say I suffered from culture shock. I'll admit I looked out of place to New Yorkers who were probably seeing their first Nebraskan in flannel shirts. OK, call it a draw – there was enough culture shock to go around!

It was a one-year program with job interviews starting in the fall. However, there was one big roadblock – the program was very difficult and each class had only a single exam at semester's end. I didn't have time to interview; I had to study just to survive. But then I saw a sign-up sheet for some tax judges who were visiting from Washington, D.C. After being invited back for second interviews, I had three judges telling me that now-familiar story: it came down to a choice between me and "one other person." I couldn't believe it. I was sure the "other person" already had a job! And of course, true to form, the first two judges picked the "other" person. Miraculously though, my luck finally changed and the last judge with whom I interviewed offered me a job.

Finally, my job search that started in college had ended. I was twenty-six. After six years of searching, interviewing and being rejected more times than I could count, I'd landed a job!

LESSONS LEARNED LATE:

- Aim high – set the highest job goal possible.

- See things clearly – rejection is a fact, and it's not personal.

- When you interview, look like them, dress like them and talk like them (they want to hire more of them).

- Thank you letters are important. A brief, handwritten, note is a powerful, lost art.

- Learn something positive each time you're turned down (there are often clues about why you were rejected that can serve as building blocks for future success).

- As the rejections pile up, don't panic. Remember, you only want to find one job.

- Persistence pays. Hold out as long as you possibly can (and outlast the other job seekers), because years later, when you're working at that one great job (the one you aimed high for), you can look back on that long, tough, lonely road and smile.

- Maybe you shouldn't be an employee. Maybe you should be an entrepreneur and start your own business.

3. GUT CHECK: WITH CHOICES, HOW DO YOU MAKE THE DECISION?

As I look back over my life, I've made many mistakes. Some big, some small. My mistakes can be put into two categories. There were those decisions I made with the best information available and with the best of intentions. As my life played out, for a variety of reasons, my decisions proved to be on the "wrong" side of the ledger. I don't view any of these decisions with regret. I tried to think things through to the best of my ability, and then the other forces of life took over. Sometimes you win and often times you lose. It's just the way life works out. I accept it and wouldn't try to change any of these decisions because I tried my best at that moment and things just didn't work out. You take your lumps and move on.

There is a second and smaller category of decisions that I do regret. I don't regret that they didn't turn out the way I wanted because I'm philosophical about life. I'm a positive person and I like to expend my energy looking forward. I like to live life looking out the windshield and not in the rearview mirror. I don't regret how they turned out, necessarily, but how I made them. With these decisions, I didn't follow my gut instincts. My gut was telling me "no" but others were telling me "yes." My stomach was churning at the time while I was fighting my gut and I eventually gave in and decided to follow the voices of others. These were big decisions about relationships and job offers. One decision in particular was so "wrong" for me, that I developed a wrenching muscle spasm in my lower back. It hurt so bad that I couldn't even sit in a car. The amazing part? I was in excellent shape and had never experienced a back problem in my life. I'm convinced it was psychological. I was so stressed that I worked myself into physical pain. The message? Follow your gut instincts or your future will be in peril.

How should you make "major" decisions in your life, especially those about your job or career? By listening to your gut instincts. Some say your "alarm bells" go off, some call it following your "true north," and I suspect the experts would describe it as a state of cognitive dissonance. Whatever it's called, you know exactly what I'm talking about because you've experienced it in your own life. You've ignored your gut just like me and with the same results. Your gut was leading you in the right direction, but those voices, yours and others, chatted away and convinced you otherwise. Oh my!

As I've walked through life, I've tried to separate "regular" decisions from "big" decisions. The "big" ones are those that are either obviously big (a new job, moving to a new city) or those that foreclose other choices down the road. For example, as a sophomore in college, I decided I needed to "kick myself in gear" because if I didn't raise my grade average, I would not qualify for graduate school. Thus, no grades, no future choices. A low grade point would foreclose all of those options. Not a good decision and I realized it in the nick of time. It is these "big" choices that require extra time and thought. They require that you pay special attention to your gut. Ignore it at your peril. I can't explain why, but I can tell you my gut has a one hundred percent "accuracy rating." I bet yours does too.

If you and I both know from experience that our gut leads us in the right direction, then why don't we always follow it? Why isn't life this simple? Because it takes courage to follow your gut instinct. Our gut tells us what's "right deep down" and for a variety of reasons we don't want to listen. Our gut choice is often the unpopular one at the moment. It may cost us a relationship, it may cost us our friends and/or it may require that we not "follow the crowd." What fun is that? None at all in the short-term. In fact, following our gut may deny us short-term pleasure and require long-term pain for long-term gain. It may require that we follow a path of patience, hard work and delayed gratification. In our world of instant gratification, who wants to wait?

LESSONS LEARNED LATE:

- Separate big decisions from small ones.
- Big ones include choices made today that will foreclose future opportunities.
- Listen to what your gut is telling you and figure out why.
- Call your good friends and seek their counsel.
- Follow your gut instincts.
- This will take courage.
- The "gut instinct" choice may require that you follow a path of patience, hard work and delayed gratification.
- Over time, you will find your authentic inner voice.
- Ignore your gut at your peril.
- Once a decision is made, don't look back.
- Live life looking through the windshield and not through the rearview mirror.

4. GETTING THE JOB WAS JUST THE AUDITION: NOW THE SHOW BEGINS

Following my work for the Judge, I got a job as a lawyer with a law firm. After only a few weeks, I discovered that law firms do at least one thing well. They guarantee new hires a place to start at the bottom. While made up of individual lawyers with different specialties, there is a clear, if unwritten, "chain of command." Everyone above you has first choice. You can be certain someone else will grab the plum assignments. Even if they somehow get stuck with the clunker of a case or project, they are eager to hand it off to the new hire. I also realized that, in the grand scheme of things, young lawyers don't know very much. They are, therefore, "fungible" worker bees. A newly hired lawyer is a person with the perfect combination of no practical knowledge plus inexperience, thereby insuring that the worst assignments will land on their desks.

I aspired to be a "corporate" tax lawyer. They were the ones involved in the deals you'd read about in the business section of the newspaper. I imagined working well into the night on a takeover, merger or IPO that was the talk of the business community. I was sure I'd be power lunching with corporate executives in no time. However, as my track might have predicted, that was not exactly how it turned out. When the "big deals" came along, the senior lawyers kept that work for themselves.

What was left? Bankruptcies. Yes, as usual, my timing was perfect. The economy had just taken a turn for the worst. The firm had lots of bankruptcy projects and since I was the last tax guy hired for more than three years, I got to spend even more time at the bottom. In the back of my mind, I always wondered why the firm bothered with this sort of work. Weren't these companies bankrupt because they didn't have enough money? And if they'd already run out of money, what was the upside? What was I missing here?

My first bankruptcy case proved to be my most memorable. After only a few weeks at the firm, a third-year trial lawyer walked into my window-less office unannounced and told me to report to his office immediately. I was hesitant, because I was sure the law firm had an assignment list (with employee preferences!), but he quickly disabused me of that notion. I had little respect for him, because he obviously was a bottom-dweller just like me. As I walked into his office, he told me he needed my help on a tax case that was set to go to trial before a bankruptcy judge. Dutifully, I pulled out a legal pad (that's about the only thing a new lawyer knows how to do – write notes on a legal pad) and asked him to give me the facts.

After he explained the background, it was obvious this case was a loser. I asked, "So, what's the issue?" He explained that Mr. Smith had met an untimely demise while owing back taxes and left his widow to defend his actions against the government. We had been appointed to represent the widow. Incredulous, I said, "So, what's the issue?" He looked me straight in the eye and said we had to win this thing. I then asked, "How are you going to do that?" He replied, "I don't know. That's why you're here – now get out of my office and go figure it out!"

Working continuously day and night (fear of failure is a powerful motivator), I came up with some novel theories. I didn't know if they'd work, but that didn't seem to bother the young trial lawyer. He explained that a "good" lawyer can figure out three ways to lose a case, but a "really smart" lawyer can figure out an additional five. That adds up to a total of eight ways to lose. He, on the other hand, didn't want to hear about how tough the case was, how impossible the odds or how many ways we could lose. No, what he demanded was the one way the case could be won. Simply, neither giving in nor losing was an option. He would think in such creative ways, sometimes even turning the case "upside down," until he would figure out a winning strategy. Even if it was a long shot, he would pursue the strategy with a passion like nothing I'd seen before (or since, for that matter).

What happened with the case? Well, that could the subject of another book. Suffice it to say that we successfully defended the widow and she wrote a hand-written note thanking my friend for his passionate representation. As for he and I, our friendship flourished and he asked me to be his best man when he got married. To this day, he's one of my most trusted friends. When we talk, infrequently, how do we end the call? "I love you, buddy."

LESSONS LEARNED LATE:

- Starting at the bottom breeds a lifetime of humility.

- Be a positive employee your employer can't live without.

- The only option is to find the one way to win (a task that's harder than it appears).

- With clarity, define what "winning" looks like at the start of a case or project.

- Never give up. Never give in. Sometimes, your determination will be the only thing you have going for you.

- Break the most complex project down into many simple components (Dad would say "There are no complicated tasks, just a greater series of simple ones").

- When you finally talk to the judge (or audience), imagine you've already won and speak with absolute conviction. Remember, a judge must be convinced you're convinced, and will prod for any sign of weakness.

5. TOUGH + LOVE

When I finally started working as a lawyer, I was not tough. I did not have a clue what "tough" was. In fact, whatever the opposite of tough was, that would've been me. Being from Nebraska, I saw the world in simple terms. I had no understanding of human nature and the dynamics in the workplace. I had no understanding of a world occupied by adversaries. I thought everybody told the truth, did what they said they'd do and put in a day's work for a day's pay. I thought everybody played by the same rules and would abide by them. In addition, and to make matters worse, I wanted to be liked.

I thought if I worked hard and did my best, my work would speak for itself and my career would progress in a linear path upward. It just had to work that way, didn't it? Boy, was I wrong! I wasn't proved wrong slowly, either, but with lightning quick speed. It was an instant shock to my system and something I had to come to grips with in a hurry. Within weeks, my entire future, indeed, my entire career hung in the balance.

What I discovered (not gently mind you, more like getting hit in the face with a shovel) was that there are people in the world with different value systems, different priorities and different agendas. It's not homogonous. These people are motivated by their own self-interests. At any moment in time, their self-interests are either aligned with yours (unlikely, and a small group to be sure), unaligned with yours (which means they truly don't care about you), or in direct opposition to yours (you're in the way and they need to run over you to get what they want). This means that only a small percentage of people are aligned with you and want to make decisions in support of you. Most truly don't care and are not going to expend any energy to help you. Then, there are those who have identified you as "being in their way" and they will expend the energy to push you aside. You are on the radar screen and they have every motivation to run over you. Who are "those people" I'm speaking about? Virtually everyone you come into contact with, whether co-worker, competitor, adversary or person you need to convince to make the sale (called "customers" or "clients" I believe).

Of course, I would be taught this lesson immediately at the start of my career under the harshest of circumstances. I believe it is commonly referred to as "trial by fire." My first case given to me by a young trial lawyer involved us defending a widow against the Internal Revenue Service. I don't believe I'm overstating when I say the IRS is one of the most feared adversaries. They wanted to win their case and collect the taxes they believed were owed. After only a few weeks on the job, I'd been "drafted" to go to the front lines and defend the case against none other than the IRS. No, it was even worse than that. Mere "defending" was not acceptable. I was being told by the young trial lawyer (who was supposed to be on my side!) that, "we had to win this thing." Nothing less would be tolerated, discussed or accepted. All I could think about was "how on earth did I manage to get myself into this mess?" Far more worrisome, how was I going to get me and my client out of it? Is crying allowed in law firms?

I lived with a pit in my stomach for almost three years. When I'd confess to my colleague "I can't do it," he would lecture me to "get tough." When I told him the case was overwhelming and I was worried he would say, "So, do you just want to quit and lose today? Is that what we're going to do?" Answering his own question, he'd say "No, that's not an option." He never backed down or backed off and he wouldn't let me either. He believed "weakness" and "winning" could never exist in the same sentence. He believed in me when I didn't believe in myself. To bring me along, it was like he filled my "tough tank" up a little at a time, and on the fly.

We each need to "get tough." Why? Because the opposite of a life of toughness is a life of worry. Worry is a draining, negative energy that can't help you solve a problem, complete a project or win a case. Talk to any successful athlete or coach and they've never used worry to succeed in their careers, win a competition or reach and maintain a maximum performance level. Call my friend the trial lawyer (he's now a "big dog") and ask how many cases he's won with worry. For those doubters, let me ask a question: how many things that you've worried about have come true? How many things that you've worried about one day have become reality the next?

In my life, the answer is "not many" and I suspect the same is true for you. So, fill up your "tough tank" and get on with your wonderful life. This will be of great benefit and solace when you realize that, as I've mentioned above, only a few people are aligned with you, most don't care and the others think you're in the way and need to be run over. Why worry about them, when they're not worried about you?

LESSONS LEARNED LATE:

- Resolve to get tough

- Begin by filling up your tough tank

- Understand that only a few people have interests aligned with yours, most won't care and the others think you're in their way and need to be run over.

- Worry is a negative, draining energy. How many things that you've worried about, have come true?

- Has worrying helped you to accomplish something important in your life?

- Weakness and winning can never exist in the same sentence

- Luke Skywalker, "I can't believe it!" Yoda, in response: "That is why you fail!"

- Repeat after Yoda: "Do or do not. There is no try!"

6. THE KEY TO YOUR EMOTIONS IS IN YOUR HAND

(THIS KNOWLEDGE IS YOUR POWER)

So, you ask, what if you don't have your own young fire breathing trial lawyer who throws you to the wolves in order to toughen you up? What do you suggest? Besides, you say, I'm reading this book to get simple advice and battling the IRS seems far too complicated. Here's my advice on how to get personally tough against the influences of others.

Imagine your emotional state is a beautiful garden. It is lush with green plants and flowers. These plants are arranged just as you want them and are hardy but fragile. You've taken great care to create this garden, watering frequently and weeding when necessary. Realizing your garden needs protecting, you've built a fence around it. Your fence is strong and sturdy and will prevent both animals and humans from getting through. To allow visitors, which are important, you've installed a tall gate. The only way to open the gate and enter your garden is with a key, and you hold the only key in your hand.

Here's my question for you. Imagining that your beautiful garden is your delicate emotional state, your feelings, are you going to voluntarily let anyone in who will trounce your garden? Can anyone come in and step all over your plants and trample your flowers? Would you just stand there and watch as they danced with glee and destroyed your pride and joy? The answer is "absolutely not." You would never allow this to happen. You would fight to protect your beautiful plants. You would be outraged if this happened once and would resolve to never let it happen again.

My point is this. Our own emotions and feelings belong to us. The only way our feelings get hurt is if we allow it to happen. Our feelings, like an imaginary garden, deserve to be protected. We can't change the way others act, but we sure can change how we react.

More to the point, no one can hurt your feelings without your permission. Your feelings are safe behind a gate and you hold the key. This knowledge is your power. Are you going to give any idiot the key, your permission, to walk in and stomp all over your emotions? No, you should never let this happen. You should be outraged if it happens once and resolve to never let it happen again.

LESSONS LEARNED LATE:

- Imagine your emotions are like a beautiful garden, protected by a fence and an iron gate.
- You have the only key to the gate.
- No one gets in to your emotional garden without your permission.
- Resolve to never give any idiot the key, your permission, to walk in and trample your emotional garden.
- This knowledge is your power.
- Post a "Go Away" sign to any idiot who keeps trying to get in.
- Live a great life of tough + love, with your emotions protected.

7. THE NOT SO SMALL THINGS MATTER

A. Character

We all know that character matters. Everyone who comes into contact with you will be judging your character. Your supervisor, your subordinates and even your adversary will be acutely attuned to how you act and how you define and respect limits. It's your currency that will add to your goodwill in the workplace. But what is it? How would you define "character" so that it's meaningful? I like this definition: "Character is what you do when no one is looking and you're sure you'll never get caught."

Character is evident at both big moments and small ones. Are you truly a person of integrity who lives it on a daily basis? What do you do when no one's looking? And, at the other extreme, how far will you go to do things right and make things right?

Character can be hidden, glossed over or ignored during the good times. However, a person's character will be fully revealed when adversity sets in. When the heat gets turned up, the pressure builds and a deadline looms, how will you react? Will you be a person that runs, hides or blames others? Or will you rise above the moment and find clarity? As a situation gets worse, does your blood pressure go down? Do you have the ability to think more clearly in times of stress? And if things go wrong, will you be accountable, accept responsibility and even apologize to your clients or colleagues? Everyone around you is watching for this litmus test that we must face. Adversity is inevitable, so anticipate the situation and rehearse your response.

LESSON LEARNED LATE:

- Character is what you do when no one's looking and you're sure you'll never get caught.

- Adversity doesn't build character, it reveals character.

- Can you think more clearly in times of stress?

- Anticipate moments of adversity and rehearse your response.

- Sincere apologies in the workplace are powerful.

- Be accountable.

B. Speaking

i. Public Speaking

You have a pit in your stomach. You have almost worried yourself sick. Like a shadow, your fear has followed you everywhere. There's no escape and no end in sight. Is it the equivalent of a pending "trial of the century," perhaps, with you as lead counsel? Nope, not nearly so grandiose. Your boss has asked you to give a speech next month before twenty of your colleagues. A speech ... in public! How could you have gotten yourself into this awful position? And how will you ever get yourself out?

To this day, the notion of public speaking instills a powerful and unique fear. A fear that paralyzes even the most accomplished among us. There's good news. You are not the first person to stand up in public and give a speech. In fact, there are millions of similarly terrified people who've gone before you. They each survived the experience and you can too!

You've been asked to speak because you know something about the subject matter. You have the knowledge or information at hand and are being asked to present it before a group. This immediately gives you a head start on the presentation and means that you know more about the subject matter than the audience does. As you dig into the details, your command of the subject matter will rapidly increase and you'll become more curious about the fine points and areas that are unresolved. About a week before the speech, your head will be filled with details and you'll believe that your audience needs to hear it all. After all, you assume they need the details too and need to hear everything that you've learned about the subject. They must be made aware of every fact, no matter how small, right? Plus, if you can talk fast and spew out a lot of data, you'll be sure to impress them with your intelligence. The audience will walk away "wowed" with your smarts. Isn't that the goal of public speaking — to look smart?

This is the most important question you can ask yourself when preparing for a speech. My answer is no, I've never been successful at giving that type of speech. If your purpose is to communicate a body of knowledge to the audience, so that, at the end, they understand the message, then there's only one way to speak: simply, with large frames of reference. The truth is that humans hear slowly. Our other senses can process a lot of information, but our ears have a hard time keeping up. If the listener is lost, our thoughts will lead us to other places. It's called daydreaming and we all do it.

The speaker is a guest of the audience. The audience is giving you a gift of their time and you must use it wisely and maximize the impact. If you know this to be true, then why not use it to your advantage? Why not be remembered as a great communicator? Is it really that hard? No! After all, the bar is set low, my friends!

A great speech is easy to give. It can be broken down into "threes." There are three parts: an introduction, the main body, and a conclusion. An introduction starts with either a "Thank you for inviting me to be here with you today and the topic is ..." or "I've been asked to present on the subject of ..." Then provide some context, explaining why this topic is relevant or important to the audience. Then tell them that you have three main points and you can also hint at the conclusion. Lately, I've reduced it to this level of simplicity: "Please take out a pen and paper and write these three things down – these points are important and I want you to remember them." I completely eliminate the mystery and provide a context they can relate to throughout my speech.

The main body of a great speech has three points. It has three because the human ear is slow and can't remember a lot of data. So, help the audience – they are desperate to learn and want to understand. Breaking it down to three points also forces you to sift through all the raw data and make sense of it. What's really important? If you could divide the information into three "buckets," what would they be? Sometimes it's easier and sometimes it's difficult, but your audience is counting on you to do this job for them.

A great conclusion can begin with "In conclusion" or "Now, I'd like to conclude my remarks." These words give the audience a clue that you are changing gears and heading toward the finish. A great conclusion will repeat the topic or purpose for the speech, remind the audience of the three points discussed in the body and then will either ask them to do something (decide, vote, etc.) or simply thank them for their time and the opportunity to speak before them today. Often, you will turn the meeting back over to the leader/moderator for further proceedings.

A great speech has a few other ingredients. The tone of your voice, eye contact and body movements are just as much a part of your speech as your words are. Have a strong tone, remember to make eye contact and stand with your feet still. Hand gestures are good for emphasis, but your movement should be kept to a minimum or be strategic and purposeful. During the speech, there are three things I remind myself: (1) breathe; (2) it's good to fill up transitions with silence (and not with "uhs" or other filler words); and (3) speak with a leader's voice. Breathing is especially important because it will help you to relax and slow the pace of your words.

All great speeches have one other thing in common: practice. No matter how experienced, you must practice the speech and do so repeatedly. In sports, a Coach will say "You play like you practice" and that applies equally to public speaking. Practice in front of a mirror or even in front of friends or family. If the speech is important to your career, "test drive" the speech in front of a close friend/colleague at work to make sure the words and tone are appropriate. For the big ones, arrive at the venue early and get accustomed to the lectern, microphone set-up and audience seating. Be prepared for things to go wrong during your speech. I always bring a printed copy of my slides in case there are problems with the computer or projector. Instead of apologizing, resolve to be unflappable. The audience just wants to hear your presentation and understands when problems occur.

LESSONS LEARNED LATE:

- You've been asked to speak because others think you have the knowledge. Build on that vote of confidence.

- A great speech is easy to give.

- There are three parts: introduction; main body (with three points/topics); and conclusion.

- In the introduction, provide context and tell them what you are going to say.

- In the body, repeat the three points/topics.

- In the conclusion, summarize the three points and, if the purpose is a call to action, then ask them to decide, vote, etc.

- Breathe and embrace silence.

- Speak with a leader's voice.

- Practice many times.

- Be prepared for things to go wrong during your speech. Resolve to be unflappable.

- Smile and enjoy the show!

ii. Private Speaking

The shelves of bookstores are filled with books on the topic of public speaking. But I haven't seen much written on the subject of private speaking (though admittedly, I haven't been paying attention). By this, I mean the everyday communication that fills our days at work. It's talking with a client, chatting with a colleague or speaking up in a meeting.

It's difficult to change our speaking patterns because we're largely unaware of them. How do we sound to others? Is it possible that the entire subject of private speaking could be distilled into a paragraph or, better yet, a sentence? I believe so and would like to give it a try.

My advice: Speak with a leader's voice. This phrase is powerful because we know what leader's do and don't do. They don't whine, complain, blame or demean others. They speak calmly and with conviction and make eye contact. They talk about the possibilities of success and not the many ways to fail. They speak clearly using simple, persuasive words. The good ones avoid "buzz" words or "corporate speak." When a leader is finished, you want to jump on board and become part of the solution. It seems effortless.

Over time, you too can speak like a leader. If you do, it will have a powerful, positive impact on your career.

LESSONS LEARNED LATE:

- Challenge yourself to become a better speaker today.
- Prepare, practice and simplify your words.
- How do you sound to others?
- Resolve to speak with a leader's voice.

C. Writing

When I started law school, I found myself bombarded by an avalanche of new words. Some were really old, some were Latin and some sounded like they shouldn't be repeated in public (try "fiduciary"). The same is true, of course, of any profession and most industries. Since you've endured the pain of learning these words, you are eager to try them out on others. It separates you from the crowd and makes you look smart. I thought I knew how to write well and was eager to add new words to my arsenal. Imagine the fun of writing the word "fiduciary" and getting paid for it!

Once again, I received a rude awakening. I had a law professor who did two things. First, he challenged me to build an ever-expanding vocabulary. Second, he made it clear that using big words was neither good nor tolerable. He said this: Write clearly and simply. "Lawyer" words should never be used whenever a simple word will do. Then he applied this lesson to me with a vengeance. He corrected me, ordering me to rewrite my papers. He was relentless and unapologetic. It was a lesson I needed to learn and I'm thankful to this day that he cared enough to take the time to correct me.

Why is this discussion of writing necessary or relevant? "I already know more than I want to about this subject," you may say. Because there's a new enemy of good writing: it's called email. It seems that every fundamental lesson we learned about writing has been thrown out the window. An email message is a license to say whatever you want, however you want, with as little punctuation as possible. It's like we're all chatting and writing down whatever pours out.

My advice: words can never be taken back, so choose them carefully. Write simply and use complete sentences with punctuation. Always review and edit one last time before you hit "send." I'm always thankful later for the deletion of those extra words or sentences that really weren't necessary. Your messages will be pleasing to the eye and command respect. There is one more perspective to offer. A lawyer friend once remarked: "I always read my email messages twice before I hit send. Once for content and the second time to see how it sounds if it were someday read to the Grand Jury!" Yikes!

LESSONS LEARNED LATE:

- Write clearly and simply.

- Make sure you possess a large vocabulary that's never used.

- Avoid the use of "big" words, when a simple one will do.

- Follow Mark Twain's advice: "I'd have written less if I had more time."

- Email messages should be concise, with complete sentences and punctuation. If you are asking permission or a question, make sure the question is clearly stated. What do you want the recipient to do?

- Read an email message you are drafting twice – the second time out loud.

- Edit one more time before you hit "send" (you'll always be thankful for this last step).

- Respect must be earned before it can be received.

D. Body Language

We convey most information about ourselves through our body language. Unless we are trained, most of us cannot suppress the many ways in which our inner feelings "leak out." What does your body language convey about you? How might that language be changed to convey a new, more confident, you?

Let's take a simple example. When you walk into a room, what does your posture say about you? When you are walking down a hallway towards a colleague, what does she see? If your shoulders are slumped or you have even slightly poor posture, are your words going to have their maximum persuasive value? If you are selling your ideas or asking a group to agree with your recommendation, and it's a close call, don't you need everything to work in your favor? Stated differently, are you unconsciously sabotaging your career?

On the subject of posture, consider this example. Standing near me in an electronics store was a twenty year-old boy waiting to ask the salesman questions. He had the face of a kid and his buddies looked even younger. When he spoke, he had the voice of a kid and asked the questions a kid would ask. However, there was something very different about him. When he walked towards me down the aisle, I could see that he carried himself with confidence and composure. Making small talk, the salesman asked what he did and he responded that he was in the military. What branch? He replied "USMC, Sir." This kid was no kid. He was a Marine. And when he walked, his posture spoke volumes. He had an unmistakable air of confidence, readiness and respect. His body language conveyed that he both gave and commanded respect. Next time you see a Marine, focus on his/her posture. And if he/she shows up for a job interview, you can be sure they'll get the offer. There is much for us to learn from the military.

LESSONS LEARNED LATE:

- What does your body language convey about you?
- Are your shoulders slumped or do you have poor posture?
- Are you unconsciously sabotaging your career?
- How could your body language be changed to convey a new, more confident, you?
- Imagine walking with an unmistakable air of confidence, readiness and respect.

8. THE CHARACTERISTICS THAT GET YOU PROMOTED, SERVE YOU SO POORLY ONCE YOU GET THERE

Not that I've been promoted much (or often, for that matter!), but it took me years to figure out that the characteristics that get you promoted serve you so poorly in your next position. As a young lawyer, you are good at doing what you're told and researching and writing memos. That means you develop the skills of narrow and patterned thinking as you read books, statutes and judicial decisions and then write the obligatory memoranda. Later, a young lawyer progresses to either drafting court pleadings (if a litigator) or documents (if a business lawyer). These pleadings and documents can be long and detailed, requiring immense concentration. These tasks combine to produce a mid-level associate who "knows a lot about a little" and has an incredible eye for detail. With page after page of proverbial "fine print" the lawyer must both understand the words written and make sure the "deal terms" or facts are all included. The documents must be constantly scoured for "typos" and errors. In the final rush towards trial or the closing of the deal, you only hope and pray that the documents are accurate and mistake-free.

After mastering a narrow area of the law and the art of producing voluminous documents (the joke is that lawyers get paid by the pound!), the not-so-young lawyer is promoted to a supervisory role and, hopefully, to partner. This pattern occurs in most professions and industries. In business, a staff person gets promoted to manager and then on to lead a team. On what basis is the promotion made? Typically, on the basis of how well you performed in your "old" job of being a "hands on" detail-oriented person. In that role, you were solely responsible for the tasks performed and had a sense of being "in control." You read every document and personally completed every task. You didn't need to trust other co-workers, because the project, by definition, was not completed until you had personally completed every step. At this level, I could imagine every such employee/professional writing a book titled "Micro Managing Made Easy!" Further, if you told them they would write such a book at this stage of their career, they are so myopic they wouldn't even get the joke! "What's so funny? Micromanaging is what I do best! Is there any other way?"

Then you get promoted and you are assigned multiple projects with multiple teams. You must both manage and lead others, sometimes by guidance, sometimes by inspiration and every so often by orders. You must become a strategic thinker and spend time "thinking big." It's that "vision thing" that must occupy your waking moments. Your people skills will be severely tested, both with your own team and with your clients/customers. Your ability to focus on the details and a single task at hand becomes the enemy of the skills required to perform your new responsibilities. So, your "instincts" are pointed in the wrong direction and your considerable skills will serve you poorly. Detail-oriented micromanager is the polar opposite of trusting/inspiring team leader. You will quickly realize that there aren't enough hours in the day to read everything and do every task performed by those under you. A difficult and uncomfortable feeling will swallow you up. Oh my gosh, I must give broad tasks to others and then trust they will get the job done right. How do I re-train myself and learn the new skills necessary to be a successful leader?

Like anyone with a "problem," the first step is to admit it. In this case, the challenge is to recognize that your old skills will not serve you well and you need to quickly develop new ones that match the demands of your new job. Your technical abilities/knowledge are not as important as your ability to see the big picture, set priorities, define success, create accountability and manage and motivate others. Further, your future success will depend not on your ability to see the world internally, through your eyes, but externally through the eyes of your customers/clients. You will be shocked to learn that they don't care about your problems. They have their own and you exist, if at all, to help them solve their problems. It's not about what you have to sell, it's only about what your customers need to succeed. The more adept you are at putting yourself in your customer's shoes, learning about their business and finding out what their current challenges/problems are, the more successful you'll be. Of course, you can stay internally focused and never advance in your career or, worse yet, learn that your competitor has become your customer's trusted advisor. Needless to say, not a good answer!

A great place to start is to read business books on strategy, leadership and how to "think like a customer." It is even more important to find great mentors. I use the plural, because you should be collecting mentors at each stage of your career and they should be both inside and outside your company/firm. An "inside" mentor is someone you respect who's been in your position before and can help you navigate the culture of your company and provide suggestions for your personal growth. Find this person and ask them questions. Ask for their advice, and you'll be amazed at the positive response. You should also find a mentor outside of your company who can give you a "big picture" perspective and career counseling advice. This person can provide the "unvarnished" truth about you and your career. Since they don't have any company bias, their perspectives will be invaluable. For example, ask them what are the three lessons they learned early in their careers and ask what are three things you should be doing to advance your career. The advice will be priceless. After getting great advice from your mentors, your next job is to "pass it on," and be a great mentor to those who follow you. A task a little tougher than it appears.

LESSONS LEARNED LATE:

- The skills that get you promoted will serve you so poorly once you get there.

- Identify and learn the new skills necessary to your future success. Quickly.

- Start developing these two skills: Be a leader and inspire others.

- See the world through the eyes of your clients. Think like a buyer.

- Be a trusted advisor (or your competitor will fill the void).

- Find great mentors and ask for their advice in "threes."

- Advice from a mentor is priceless.

- Repay the favor. Find a person to mentor and make them a priority.

9. A FEAR WE SHARE: THE FEAR OF SUCCESS

I'm sure you're familiar with the fear of failure. It's a fear that has two sides. It can be destructive, but it can also be constructive. In it's destructive form, it prevents you from entering the race. Why even attempt to do something when you know you're doomed to fail. It is a common and powerful fear, to be sure. It prevents many from trying something new or venturing out into unknown territory. On the other hand, it can prove to be a powerful motivator. A fear of failure can stick in the back of your mind and make you work that much harder. You're convinced that if you don't work your "tail off," you might fail. Since that's a terrible result to avoided at all costs, you go the "extra mile" to make sure there's little chance of failing.

From my experience, the fear of failure is clear to identify and relatively easy to deal with. When a person has a fear of failure, they often won't even try and will just walk away. Friends and colleagues who know the person will notice and ask some questions. Since we're all familiar with this fear, we can easily empathize and offer encouragement. I'm sure this goes back to our shared childhood experiences of being afraid of some activity or falling off something. Whatever it is, we've all encouraged someone with the words "Come on, try it! You can do it!" With a little coaxing, the fear is overcome and the activity enjoyed by all.

I believe there's another, more problematic, fear. It's far more subtle. It has only a negative consequence on a person's behavior. It can't be used to motivate. I call it the fear of success. Again, I'm no expert and certainly not a trained psychologist, but I've experienced this fear in my life and for many years it was a powerful inhibitor. It prevented me from reaching my potential and held me back.

For me, it worked like this. I would make about a seventy percent effort in school. This level of effort gave me a "comfort zone." It was enough effort to get a fairly good grade, let's say a "B," but not good enough to excel. It worked for me because if I gave a 100% effort, and then I didn't get a good grade, then I'd know I'd failed for sure. If I gave a subject or class my maximum effort and then got a low grade, I really had failed and there was no excuse. In my system, if I didn't really try, then I never actually failed because in the back of my mind I always had an excuse. It might sound a little nutty, and certainly self-defeating, but I've seen it in myself and in many others.

Without maximum effort, I was sabotaging my own intellectual growth and progress. I was giving myself a seventy percent education with seventy percent results. I continued, more or less, on this path until I left home and moved to New York City to attend New York University. I had no idea how hard the program would be. After only two weeks of classes, I was in a dual state of despair and depression. The other one hundred fifty students were lawyers who had done well in law school, passed the bar exam and then decided to concentrate their studies for one more year. They were motivated to be there and well prepared for the task. I was not prepared for the rigors of such a school, and was shocked at the educational prowess of my classmates. They all seemed so confident and so prepared.

The professors would call on us daily (we had "problems" that had to be analyzed and answered in order to be prepared for each two hour class) and everyone else knew the answers. Between classes, all of the NYU students would congregate in the student lounge and I would over-hear them talking about where they went to college. Worse, they would connect on the basis of where they went to summer camp. "I went to Camp Chip-A-Tooth, too!" they would say with glee! As for me, I'd never heard of summer camp before. In fact, growing up in Nebraska, I guess it could be said I had an advantage because my entire life was a summer camp! A roll in the hay field or a dunk in the farm pond was just down the street! What's the big deal? And why would your parents pay for such a thing?

But the sand had run out of my hourglass. It was midnight and "poof" I was a pumpkin. For the first time in my life I was in a panic and faced with the ultimate challenge. Either I could just quit in September and return to Nebraska with nothing to show for it (and my tuition money lost), or, I could give it my 100% maximum effort. Such an effort would require that I study day and night for the next four months and roll the dice. Even if I gave the total effort, there was no assurance I would pass. Even if I stayed, the result might be the same.

I mulled this over for a week and then it hit me. I needed to face my fears and give it my all. I needed to live my life without regrets and if I quit I'd regret that decision for the rest of my life. I would condemn myself to a life filled with self-doubt and "what if's." The consequences of quitting were far worse, as it turned out, than the consequences of staying and flunking out. I'd never quit on anything in my life and now was not the time to start. So, I lived and breathed school and committed to give an unconditional, no excuse, and maximum effort. I decided to study every day and every night, and I did it. As the initial weeks passed, it didn't seem so bad, because I was a starving student without any money, so what's the difference?

To make matters worse, the exams were after the Christmas holidays. So, I spent that holiday season looking out my window at the beautiful lights of New York. By this time, I was numb (not dumb!). I was in a fog produced by too many tax laws for any one person to handle. One by one, I took each exam. I was surprised to find they were "open book." But, as any student knows, that's a cruel joke played by the professors, because if you didn't know the answer, you were in big trouble. There were too many questions and too little time given to answer them even if you wrote like crazy. There was no time to look anything up. My books and notes just sat there in a lump.

After a short break, I returned for the second semester and the grades were slowly posted. I got a "B" on my first grade and I was thrilled. That "B" meant I hadn't flunked out. I had no expectations for the other grades, just total relief knowing I'd not have to move back to Nebraska embarrassed. Turned out that, to my shock, my first grade was my lowest and, by any measure, I'd risked everything and won. My fear of success was crushed.

Have you experienced the fear of success in your life? Have you possibly seen it manifest itself in the lives of others? It can be subtle, but it's real. The shame is that it might not be recognized and help, support and encouragement given in time. I encourage you to face it and face your challenges with maximum effort. Don't live with any regrets. Don't sabotage your life. I don't believe that giving something a one hundred percent effort can ever be called "failure." A life well lived requires courage and risk. Interestingly, such a life does not require "success" at every turn.

LESSONS LEARNED LATE:

- The fear of failure is something we're familiar with. It might even be a positive force in your life.

- The fear of success is more subtle. It gives you the comfort of a ready-made excuse.

- You'll be protected from failure when you never unconditionally reach for success.

- Stop sabotaging your life and your career. Resolve to risk and reach for the high bar.

- A life well lived requires courage. No regrets.

- You can either follow your fears or be led by your passions.

10. WHEN YOU TRAVEL, HAND YOUR MONEY OVER

A. Tip Well

I learned the importance of tipping from a great boss. He led by example and never imposed his way of doing things on his subordinates. But he sure had a lot to offer, if you'd just ask. He believed tipping well was a priority dictated from two different perspectives. The individuals who serve you do so because they like people. If they do their job of pleasing you, the customer, well, why shouldn't they be paid extra for it? Why shouldn't their pay be commensurate with their effort? The other perspective was equally compelling: a service person makes only a small wage and depends on tips for their livelihood. They need the money more than you do. So, give it to those who earn it and who need it. After all, they are waiting on you. Plus, tipping generously is further evidence of living a life of gratitude for the blessings you've received.

B. Give to the Poor

I learned this lesson from a friend whose name and company you'd recognize. We were discussing our travels, particularly to New York City. I remarked about the increasing number of poor people begging on the street. He agreed. Then he said something surprising. He said he took it as an opportunity to help them. He made it a point to have extra cash in his pocket so that he could give it away. When someone approached him and asked for money, he would pull the bills from his front pocket and hand them over. His reasoning: If someone is asking, they need help. Or to put it simply, they needed the money more than he did. And so it was.

I was awestruck. He said to me "you ought to try it." I did try it and it has added a new dimension to my life. In fact, I've been shocked by the positive affect it's had on me. There's also been a mystifying constant: the person I give money to says the same thing: "God Bless You." I can't comprehend their words to me, as they look deep into my eyes. I've already been blessed in my life. Aren't they the ones who need a blessing? I now have my own stories to tell and it has added a richness to my life that I could never have imagined. A person receives more than they give. It is also a constant reminder of the importance of humility. It could very well be me asking for money some day.

LESSONS LEARNED LATE:

- When you travel, be prepared to empty your pockets.
- Make it a priority to tip well.
- If someone asks for money, they need it more than you do.
- You will receive more than you give.
- Live a life of humility and gratitude. Give with joy.
- God Bless You.

11. IF YOU WANT TO BE REMEMBERED, DO SOMETHING MEMORABLE

In a business world filled with many faces, I want to be remembered. If I have an encounter with someone and they don't have any memory, I've failed at that moment. Over the years, I've done many things to make sure I don't fail and that I'm remembered. Here are a few and they are obvious. Except these actions must not be so obvious because when I do them I get remembered. Which makes me wonder: how can these simple, common sense actions not be commonplace?

Be Prompt. If people judge others by first impressions, then the very first impression is based on whether you're on time. In my world, being on time is a matter of respect. Do I respect the other person's time and therefore arrive promptly. Or am I late, thereby wasting the other person's time? If you are in the habit of "running behind," you will start every meeting with an apology. Is that how you want to spend the first five minutes with this important person, saying you're sorry? How many more meetings with this person do you think you'll get? If I'm meeting a client, being "on time" means arriving five minutes early. There's another benefit to "running on time" – our kids follow our lead, and what a great example to set. Being prompt is a habit that will serve them well for the rest of their life.

Be Kind to the Receptionist and Assistant. Each time I meet a receptionist or assistant, whether in person or on the phone, I always introduce myself and engage in some light conversation. It might be the weather or the traffic, but there's always something to chat about. They are the gatekeepers and I want them to immediately have a favorable impression of me. I want them to feel like they are important and respected. If they don't remember me the second time around, I've failed indeed.

Smile. I like to smile. It makes me feel better. I've found that if I smile at someone, they invariably smile back at me. That means, at that instant in time, we both feel a little better. While I haven't done the research, my experience tells me that a smiling person will be more inclined to listen to me and help me out. So if I smile and they smile back, I've immediately started a positive path towards getting what I want or need at the moment. If nothing else, I'm remembered for my smile.

Make Each Person Glad They Did Business With You. Dad was in the retail jewelry business and he repeated this phrase to me. He lived by example, and would go to great lengths to make the customer happy (and anybody else, whether it be the paper boy or his Landlord even when it was time to re-negotiate his lease). This is a lofty goal and one that's difficult to achieve. It means you start an encounter with a smile. As the conversation progresses, you are courteous and kind. You never blame, even if what they did is their fault. If you are negotiating, you make sure the result is a "win-win" scenario and not a losing proposition for their side of the deal. As an aside, you should never ask for more than you would be willing to give, if the roles were reversed. Even in the toughest of negotiations, I've never subscribed to the "get all you can" or "win at all costs" mentality.

Send Hand Written Notes. Based on my experience, and the reaction of those who've received my notes, this is a lost art. Many of my mentors encouraged me to write notes, and I would mumble with affirmative understanding. I knew I should, but I was busy and besides, what type of stationary do you use and where do you order it? Reluctantly, I started using my office stationary and hand writing in blue ink, for effect. I once wrote to an airline executive and thanked his employees for making the best out of a bad travel experience (doesn't everyone have their own "Oscar winning" tale of travel terror!). I received the most unexpected response: a letter from the executive thanking me for writing and stating the Company seldom receives a positive letter from a customer. Imagine that! An airline has thousands of employees in "customer service" and millions of customers, but their customers never say anything positive? To this day, I'm stunned by their response.

Last year, I found a stationary store (admittedly it's even easier ordering on-line) and ordered plain note cards with my name at the top. The matching envelopes have only my address on the back flap. I suspect they would be called "professional" but "understated." My goal is to send at least one hand-written (and hand addressed) note out each week. Recently, I sent one to a professional/legal publisher who deals with thousands of legal authors. He said in his twenty years, he cannot recall receiving another written thank you note from an author. He saved it and put it on his desk.

To this day, I thank my mentors for instilling this lesson. I'm confident each person who receives a note from me remembers me. Why? Because I have a distinct recollection of each person that sent a hand-written note to me (and there's not too many). Their thoughtfulness made an impact. I'm equally confident there are very few of my competitors who are doing the same.

LESSONS LEARNED LATE:

- To be remembered, you must do something memorable.
- Being "on time" means arriving five minutes early. It's a matter of respect.
- Connect on a personal level and smile.
- Make each person glad they did business with you.
- Hand written business notes are a lost art. Send a note a week.

12. MAKE FRIENDS: KEEP FRIENDS

Everyone who starts a career wants to be a success. That's why you studied hard, graduated from a great school and searched for that special job. I don't know exactly what a success is, but I know one thing it's not. Based on my experience, I don't believe a person that ends up with a pile of dough, but has no friends, can ever be called a success. May sound a little harsh and maybe I'm judgmental, but I believe that if a person has achieved every other measure of success, every standard of excellence, every career goal, that person can't be a success without friends. I also believe you earn "extra credit" in this category if you have friends collected throughout your life and from different "walks of life."

Why are friends so important? Because, you can't do it alone. Virtually everything you accomplish professionally will be done with the involvement of others. You need help. You need teammates. You need sounding boards. You need those who know you best to tell you the worst, when you need to hear the truth. Who else is up to the task? Who else is going to tell you what you don't want to hear, when you don't want to hear it? Your friends — because they don't have an agenda other than to unconditionally be there at your moment of need. They don't have an ego in the game. They're the only ones on your side and in your corner. Why? Because they are emotionally connected to you and they care deeply for your soul. They only want what's best for you and their "job" is to help you see things clearly. They see life as it is, not as you want it to be. They love you for who you are, and always will, even if there are months or years between conversations.

My friend said his dad gave him this advice: "Son, you'll be lucky to have one true friend in life. Be honored if you find one, and be an honorable friend in return." I'm sure his dad spoke for that generation, because my Dad didn't have a true lifetime friend.

On this count, I've been blessed beyond belief. I have a friend from grade school, and then friends collected throughout the levels and time periods of my life. I have best friends, but I also have many others to whom I am deeply connected. My friends have seen me at my worst and not judged me. We've shared difficult work or career experiences and never lost our connectedness earned from adversity. I can tell them anything, confide any confidence and feel safe. I love them with all my heart and they love me in return. It's unconditional "friend" love, if there is such a thing (and I know there is).

One particular joy is that my friends are different. No two are the same. One lives out West on a hill (with a breathless view), one is a retired executive who catapulted a company you've heard of into the stratosphere, one is a famous voice in Nebraska, two are prominent in the golf world (remarkably, their reputations have survived their association with me!), some are Washington lobbyists, some are teachers/professors, some are dads from my kids' school, many are fellow tax lawyers, and one is an extraordinary trial lawyer who gave me my first assignment ("win this thing!").

I'm often asked, "how do you meet/make new friends – isn't it hard?" My two part answer is (1) I don't know, and (2) maybe, but what in life worth having isn't hard to come by? And aren't things earned with effort, of more value to you? I connect with those that I feel a bond with and try to keep re-connecting whenever possible. The rest seems to take care of itself.

I met one of my dear friends while we served as judicial clerks together in Washington, D.C. In later years, I'd joke that I'm often asked why this man and I became friends, because we are different. I'd say it was easy, because we had so much in common! Let me explain. "Howard graduated from college magna cum laude with a degree in mathematical physics. I went to college! Howard went to Harvard Law School where he graduated with honors. I went to law school too! For fun, Howard played competitive bridge, learning the game from his mother, a bridge master. And, you won't believe it, I actually built a bridge in Nebraska!" With this much in common, how could we not be friends?" That rationale supported a friendship now lasting over twenty-five years. By the way, if I become a contestant on a game show, Howard will be my "phone a friend!" I can hear the question now: "The final category is mathematical physics to win the game." Howard, are you there? Answer the phone!!

LESSONS LEARNED LATE:

- Make friends during different stages of your life.

- Keep in touch with your friends. Call them for no reason. The last time you spoke, your friend told you about some important life event. Remember what it was and ask them for an update. Most often, they'll say, "Thanks for asking!"

- You'll be amazed at what they grow up to be and what they do.

- I've always been attracted to friends who were more accomplished than me. They've lived up to their billing. I've underwhelmed!

- Make new friends in your chosen field. Call them for advice. Build a network of "smarter-than-you" people.

- When a friend calls you, drop everything and make them the most important priority in your life. If a friend asks a question requiring research or follow up, do it, promptly. Never fail to get back to them within the day.

- Be the friend you'd hope to find.

13. BE AN ATHLETE FOR LIFE

What does the word "athlete" conjure in your mind? Do you picture the kids in high school who were the stars on the varsity teams? Do you think of the college athletes who are on your favorite college football or basketball teams? Or do you focus on the stars that have reached the highest level and made it to the "pros" or "big leagues?" I participated in a lot of sports as a kid, but was none of those. I wasn't the star player on any team or in any sport. I was either too short or too slow, or to be accurate, both! Like the majority of Americans, I was athletically unremarkable. I wish I could tell you a compelling story of the time I quit smoking, lost one hundred pounds and appeared in an exercise infomercial. But it didn't happen that way. For the "average" me, it was a subtle transformation.

The simple truth is, you can only think as well as you feel. If you feel lousy, you'll think lousy. If you feel tired and are out of shape, your mind will follow. Life is about quality not quantity. Life is a marathon, not a one hundred yard dash. Which means there's great news for the "rest of us." While we weren't the stars of any school team, we can be the stars of our own team. This is especially exciting when you realize that the opportunity to stay active is not reserved for the young. In fact, I believe you can be proficient in sports for your entire life. Look around and you'll see "old guys and gals" running, cycling and playing golf and tennis, just to name a few. You can continue with many sports, including endurance sports, well into your sixties and beyond. What are you waiting for?

There are many benefits to staying active. Your mind will stay sharp and focused throughout the day. You will be a great example to those around you, especially your kids. Exercise is an area of life in which you must lead by example. Isn't it great when the "old man" (literally) can hike a mountain, ride a bike or swing a club as well as the kids? Your health will improve and your eating habits will improve as well. I eat less now that I'm active for the simple reason that I understand there's a "cost" to consuming more calories. If I eat more, or eat food that I know isn't good for me, I know it'll be 15 minutes more on the exercise bike in order to work it off.

You'll meet some of the most interesting people and they'll inspire you. I've met swimmers, cyclists, runners, hikers and golfers who make me want to accomplish more in my life and get more out of life. I like being around positive people who don't brag (they do, not talk about it), don't complain or engage in self pity (I hurt my back and they said "That's no a big deal, we're all recovering from something") and are always looking for the next challenge. I've made some amazing new friends later in life, only because I decided to be active again. Simply, in all facets, the quality of my life has skyrocketed because I've decided to be an athlete for life. I'm in my mid-fifties and feel like I've turned the clock back. I've never felt better in my life. Best of all, there's nothing extraordinary about it. Nothing anyone, including you, can't easily achieve.

Consider the story of Pearl. She tried to stay fit during her life and wanted to get some exercise, but all she found were exercise videos. Unimpressed and uninspired, she decided she could "do better than that." So she started her own weekly exercise class. She's been leading her class for thirteen years. Oh, and Pearl will soon turn ninety. As reported in The Arizona Republic, "bolstered by canes, walkers and oxygen tanks, the faithful come each week to gather before Pearl …" One of her students said the "class has been a lifesaver" and "my doctor says I'm building muscle around my lungs. My life is so much better."

LESSONS LEARNED LATE:

- You can only think as well as you feel.

- Life is a marathon, not a one hundred yard dash.

- It's about quality, not quantity.

- Athletics and competition are not reserved for the young or lost with age.

- You can start being active at any age. Start tomorrow, in fact, with a five-minute walk.

- Exercise is an area of life in which you must lead by example.

- Find some activities you enjoy and pursue them with a passion.

- You'll make new friends and they'll inspire you.

- Turn back your clock.

14. BE PREPARED TO FAIL, BE FIRED, OR BOTH!

The first part of this book is devoted to finding that great job. For me, it took many years and was a study in persistence. However, life in general, and your career specifically, are not linear. It doesn't all start in the lower left hand corner and progress neatly like a gently progressing line upward towards the far upper right hand corner. Mine was filled with ups and downs and often looked like squiggles swirling around. Sometimes, I've felt like my line was going down and backwards.

Rather than the exception, I'm sure my experience is fairly typical. Seldom is your first job that "one great job" for you. You need to try things out and experience life. When you're young, you don't fully understand your own strengths and weaknesses, hopes and desires and passions that burn within you. You don't fully appreciate your talents and how they will develop on the job. It is difficult to expect that your first career choice will be your last and that you'll retire with a gold watch after forty years with the same company. In fact, it's difficult to imagine your company will survive that long, given the rapid pace of change. So, you must expect and prepare for a roller coaster ride. I'll be more direct – you must be mentally prepared to fail. In fact, if you are truly doing yourself a service, you should prepare to be fired. Wait a minute, you say! You've been a high achiever all your life. This could never happen to me!

Sorry for the reality check, but in all likelihood, you will experience one or both at some point in your career. It doesn't matter if you're a top producer, a model employee or even a coach with a winning record, there are many external forces at work beyond your control. Your company could make a series of investment decisions that seemed great at the time, but end up on the wrong end of the next market trend. Management's first response is a reduction in force, with your department eliminated. These types of job changes have nothing to do with you or your performance. It's not personal, it's business as usual. So, rather than ignore it and panic when the inevitable hits, let's discuss it up front. I learned these lessons late, but my hope is that you'll learn some of these lessons in advance.

The first thing to appreciate is the odd relationship between employee and company. One of my friends (who had many jobs with companies large and small) said that you can and must love your company, but your company can't love you back. You must give your all to the company and be willing to make personal sacrifices for the betterment of business. You must "go the extra mile" in service of your customers. Each year, you must set new and lofty goals and then work long and hard to accomplish them. Above all, you must be loyal, caring and attentive. However, the company is inanimate and is incapable of loving you back. It is incapable of making equally extraordinary efforts on your behalf. Business is a one-way street. When you think about it, this relationship is the essence of the meaning of "unrequited love." The faster you grasp this harsh reality, the better prepared you'll be to handle the "ups and downs" and stresses of business life. Viewed in this light, you'll be better positioned to manage your career more effectively.

With so much uncertainty and the pace of change increasing daily, what should you do? View your career with a healthy sense of reality and adopt a sense of urgency. Make career planning and development a top priority. If you won't do this, who will? The best way to accomplish this is to imagine you are a player's agent and the player is you. The first thing an agent does is an assessment. What are the player's strengths and weaknesses and how do those match up against the job at hand? What are you passionate about? What gets your blood flowing and causes you to speak with excitement and passion? On the other hand, what is the future of your company and the industry you're in? The agent will try to carefully match the player's skills with the needs of the team/company. The agent will also ask some big questions, like "Where do you want to be in ten years?" and what are your dreams/ambitions? Like a chef concocting a fabulous new entrée, the agent will then mix it together and produce a "recipe for success." What's yours?

A good career recipe would include the following. Find great mentors, both in your company and on the outside. It is critical to have an "outside/independent" mentor who knows you, has your best interests at heart and has no "stake in the game." This person will give you invaluable perspective and the "unvarnished truth." Meet with them periodically and ask open-ended questions, like "where do you see my company/industry going" and "what steps should I take to improve myself?" Set personal goals each year, but include personal development goals that will benefit only you. It might be joining a civic organization, taking a public speaking class or signing up for a continuing education class, but do something new each year. In your profession, be known for something. I was given this advice by a wonderful law professor, who told me to write a lengthy/seminal article and then get on the continuing education speakers circuit. I'm thankful for his advice to this day. Meet new people and expand your circle of business contacts. For example, if your business involves real estate, who are the best agents, bankers and title companies? Identify them and introduce yourself. Get them talking about their career and what advice they'd give a young person starting out and you'll be amazed at the depth of the conversation. With an eye towards job advancement or that next career, identify the job skills/training required and get started. Maybe this requires some night classes at a community college, an advanced degree or a license (securities or real estate, for example), but don't delay. Finally, update your resume periodically and refresh with new references. You never know when you might need to rush it into service!

LESSONS LEARNED LATE:

- Seldom is your first job your last.
- You may be one of the lucky few that leaves one great job for another.
- Chances are, you will fail, be fired, or both.
- Prepare yourself, in advance, for this possibility.
- You can love your company, but your company can't love you back.
- Make your career planning and development a top priority.
- Be your own agent.
- Develop your "recipe for success."
- Find and cultivate great mentors (they are invaluable).
- Set personal goals that will benefit only you.
- Identify new job skills/training and get started.
- Stay positive.
- In critical times, call your friends and ask their advice. Talk daily, if necessary.
- Be patient and hold out as long as you can for that one great (next) job.

15. RANDOM THOUGHTS ON BUSINESS

A. You're Not Perfect and Things Go Wrong

As a young lawyer, there are many forces conspiring against you. Fresh out of law school, you don't know much about how to practice law in the real world and realty provides a rude awakening. In short order, you discover the facts are elusive and adversaries are eager to run over you. A lawyer's practical life is filled with due dates and filing deadlines that encourage constant worrying. The notion of "malpractice makes perfect" was imbedded in my mind. To make matters worse, at least for me, I had to make sure that the stacks of documents I prepared or the court papers to be filed were "perfect." No mistakes, no errors, no typos (ah, the world was different before spell check). My pursuit of perfection drove me to distraction. I learned to "trust no one" and to review my work two and three times, if necessary, to find the last error that must be buried somewhere on page eighty-two or footnote two hundred. Ugh!

Over the years, I've had countless moments of stress when things went wrong and someone made a mistake. Finally, I decided I wasn't in control over the forces of the universe. It was a moment of great relief to admit that things weren't perfect and neither was I. My attitude has evolved to the point where I'm convinced things go wrong because they're supposed to! In fact, I now expect something to go wrong and am surprised only when it doesn't. I expect the unexpected. This realization is profound because it puts life in proper perspective. The sooner you realize you're not perfect and certainly not in control, the sooner you can adopt healthy coping mechanisms to deal with the inevitable. Besides, when things go sideways, you will lose your ability to "think your way out of it" if you are running around with your hair on fire. As the situation gets worse, you need to slow things down and think more clearly. As the heat in the kitchen gets hotter, are you able to get cooler? Does your blood pressure go down? Better yet, can you laugh in the face of disaster?

My personal goal is to react "calmly under fire." This allows me to be more reflective in moments of stress and to focus on the way forward. It's not about expending time and energy worrying about how I got into the mess, but about imagining creative ways to overcome the particular "speed bump" on my way to achieving a positive outcome. I've discovered that life provides challenges large and small, and it's essential to have a healthy coping mechanism ready to spring into action. Certainly, one of your most important life skills is the ability to adjust.

Lately, however, I've had my patience tested in ways I never imagined. When things go wrong, for me at least, they've gone ridiculously wrong. For example, I lived in an older house on a great lot that I planned to tear down and re-build. I was working with both the builder and the bank to get the plans just right and the financing in place. While my builder was eager to begin the demolition, he knew that nothing could be touched until the bank financing closed and the money was in hand. Unfortunately, market conditions were changing on a dime and I concluded the timing was not right for the start of this project. That morning, I received a call from my builder. "Mr. Witt, I don't know how to tell you this, but without anyone's permission, the driver of the excavator went to your house and tore it down. I was just there, and your house is a pile of rubble with a track-hoe sitting on top of it. I don't know what to say. I'm so sorry, but your house is gone!" "What," I said? "How is that possible, because I told you not to start." The builder answered sheepishly, "I know you did and I told the demo company to stop as well. But the driver didn't get the message." I was incredulous. How is it possible that you leave for work in the morning and then return that night to a home reduced to rubble? What do you do in this situation, Mr. Know-it-all? Well, my friends were of no help, because none of them had heard of someone's house being torn down. Then it hit me. I just joined the Board of a homeless shelter. I wondered if I could become the first homeless Board member to live there? Where are those homeless application forms?

B. Your People Are More Important Than Your Customers

Conventional business wisdom teaches that your customers/clients are paramount. Catchy sayings about customers are ever-present on those motivational pictures. Management spends a lot of effort reinforcing the message that customers are everything and the only thing. After all, who else but the customer will pay the bills and keep the company open for business?

I believe this singular focus on customers is misguided. While customers are the end game, your employees are the messengers. An enlightened manager will understand that a customer's experience is made memorable only because of their interaction with an employee or "team member." Business is not faceless. It's about people. A business is built, one interaction at a time, on the human spirit.

Simply, if you want your customers treated well, you better have well-treated employees. They are the face of your business and you want them smiling every time they meet a customer. Their attitude must reflect that they're glad to be working for your company and they're glad to be spending time with your customers. A positive smile radiates positive energy. It's that smile, that energy, which will keep your customers happy and back for more. Properly aligned, your goal should be to put your people first and treat them better than you treat your customers.

C. Prefer Simple

A lawyer's life revolves around complexity. In the first place, a client won't need your help if it's simple (they'll just handle it themselves). On the other hand, a lawyer is trained to look for complexity because that's where the interesting and unresolved issues are.

Clients want to know you can identify the grey areas and deal with them effectively. Plus, if you charge by the hour, you can actually get paid more if you take more time. Amazing, huh?

As I look back over the cases I've worked on, I've often achieved a good result for the client by using a simple strategy. While each matter or project starts out with complexity, the challenge is to take the complicated and try and make it simple. I'm not suggesting that you don't embrace and dig deeply into the complexity at hand. To do otherwise would be misguided. What I am saying is that my job's not complete until I can bring it back to simple. I've had better luck when I could explain, in easy to understand words, what the case was about or how the deal was structured. After all, if I can't explain it in a few words, how can I expect a Judge to understand my side of the case or the business folks to thoroughly understand the terms of their business deal? Thus, I've always been in search of, and preferred, simple.

I recently attended an executive training program at a well-known business school. To my surprise, the professors worked very hard to make their theories and teachings simple. As a group, they were brilliant and highly accomplished academicians, but individually, they used simple words and easy to understand concepts. For example, one professor/author reduced the entire subject of the execution of business strategy into three steps. First, your strategy must be simple. Second, your strategy must be specific. Third, you must be able to communicate it clearly. If you don't do these three things, what are the chances that your plan will be understood, followed and implemented? I listened and I learned. I was forever changed by their teachings, because they communicated so effectively and with such ease. With their guidance and inspiration, I've further embraced the pursuit of simple.

16. WHAT IF BEING RICH ISN'T WHAT YOU THINK IT IS?

Dad was raised on a dusty farm in Kansas. Starving at age thirteen, he walked to town and got a job so he could eat and go to school. He slept in a loft above the gas station. With survival as a priority, he didn't have much time to focus on school. Not that school wasn't important, because it was terribly so. He barely graduated from high school and often remarked that it was impossible to learn on an empty stomach. Without an education and alone, he started life's journey on a path longer and more difficult than most. As a consequence, there were many things he didn't have to help guide him through life. No college degree, no classmates to grow up with. No friends to call in a time of need, no support system to fall back on. No money in the bank for a rainy (or sunny, for that matter) day. No social standing and, even if he had, he was visibly uncomfortable in social settings, especially among groups of professional men. They intimidated him because they were educated and he wasn't. What would he talk about and why would they be interested in him?

If you made a list of life's comforts and basic necessities, Dad was forced to live without them all growing up. Knowing the hardship (which he would not openly talk about), I was struck by what he valued and what he thought was important. It could have been anything. Food and shelter. An education. A desire for social status and acceptance. Perhaps the easiest to identify would be the drive to be rich. It seems that whatever you don't have as a child, you are driven to accumulate as an adult. It would have been understandable if he spent his adult years chasing the "almighty dollar." A desire to be rich would be a powerful motivator. Being rich would provide a one-way ticket out of poverty and a rung up the social ladder. Money brings happiness, doesn't it? Or, at a minimum, it would provide a mask over the misery of his past.

Against this backdrop of having nothing and needing everything, I expected him to talk to me about the importance of money and making a buck. Being rich was a simple way out and way up. Even if he didn't have it, wouldn't that be his wish for me? Oddly, the answer was no. It's not what he talked about and it's not what he valued. Money and being rich were not the "be all and end all" of his life. What was? What would he talk about and what were his driving priorities in life. What did he value above all else? He would tell me, "Freddy, if you don't have your health, you don't have anything."

Dad was a funny creature and would do strange (I mistakenly thought they were normal) things. For one, he rarely called me. For another, when I called him, he would hang up on me. The reason? The best (and only) place to find him was at work. He would always answer the phone ("Fred Witt Jewelers!") and be happy to hear your voice. "Hey, Freddy-O, how ya doin?" But if a customer came into the store and walked up to the counter, "click" was the next thing you heard. No explanation, no goodbyes. There was no time for that. To this day, my sister and I laugh about being "hung up on" and how we are conditioned to drop the phone whenever some-one announces they need to go. As if on cue, we drop the phone instantly! No apologies needed! There was a moment in time Dad called me. It was the instant he received his test results from his annual physical. He would call and start talking: "Hi Freddy, I just got back from the doctor and everything looks good!" Then he would read the lab results! "My PSA is low," he would announce proudly! Woo Hoo! Then, invariably, a customer would walk in and he'd hang up.

We are conditioned to be striving for more and more. More money, a fancy car and a bigger house are surely required and nec-essary for a happy and fulfilling life. It's all about getting more tangi-ble signs of wealth that we can put on display. But what if happiness and wealth are not about money or stuff. What if that path is false and misleading? What if being rich isn't what we or conventional wisdom says it is?

I'm convinced that being rich largely consists of two things. The first is the ability to love and be loved. If you have a loving heart and if you live "in love," your life will be rich beyond measure. I could explain more, but you know exactly what I mean. The second is your health. Dad had a life full of things missing, including food and shelter as a child, but he told me "Freddy, if you don't have your health, you don't have anything."

Recently, I met a young doctor who works in a hospital. She was bright, articulate and thoughtful. I could tell instantly you could trust her professional skill implicitly and would be lucky to have her in your care. We talked about the pressures and rewards of professional life, and our goals and ambitions. Then, her words struck me: "But, the most important thing in life is your health. If you don't have that, nothing else will matter." She should know, because she sees patients with failing health daily. She is a witness to the gift and richness of health.

LESSONS LEARNED LATE:

- We start our careers striving to be rich.
- When referring to money, Dad would say there are two ways to be rich. Earn more or want less.
- What if being rich isn't what you think it is?
- Change your perception and value system and the riches will be yours.
- There are two things required to be rich: love + health.
- Love and be loved. Have a loving heart and live "in love."
- Health. If you don't have your health, you don't have anything.
- Start living your own life as a rich person.

PART II: RELATIONSHIPS

17. FINDING THAT SPECIAL SOMEONE

A. Unfiltered Wish List

The want ad in the personals section of the newspaper has morphed into a "profile" posted in an on-line computer-dating site. While the medium has evolved, I'm confident our "wish list" of characteristics has remained the same. Each of us has an idea about that "perfect" someone. The word that seems to capture the essence is "soul mate." I don't know what it means, exactly, and I don't know if it exists in the universe, but it sounds worthy and inspirational.

It seems that virtually all profiles describe the same person. The ad could be condensed to something like this:

> Man/Woman seeking soul mate lady/gentleman who's beautiful/handsome, kind, considerate, honest, romantic, intelligent, successful, stable (both emotionally and financially), respectful of others (but primarily me), likes to travel and visit new places (that I want to see), loves pets (mine, not yours), enjoys and is kind to children (mine, not yours), values independence (mine, not yours), and is immediately available for a long-term committed relationship (to only me) according to my pre-determined schedule (I'm looking for Mr. Right, not Mr. Right Away!). No players please!

That about captures it, don't you think? It's possible there's a few words left out of the scouting creed (thrifty, perhaps?), but doubtful.

There are at least two problems with these lists. The first is there is no filter to limit the list of words. Anything goes and everything is included. The second is this: each of us has been a part of previous failed relationships. As imperfect humans with imperfect lives, we have all been fifty percent responsible for the problems in our past. How much of a good thing can we legitimately ask for and expect in another? How much do we expect of ourselves? Are we living up to our side of the bargain? Are you the treasure you want to find?

Of course, none of this stops us from trying. And we try for a very important reason. After all, if you can't write down what you're looking for, how are you going to find it? If you rented a car in a strange city, would you drive out of the parking lot without a map and directions? No! Maybe Yogi Berra was actually providing relationship advice when he said, "If you don't know where you're going, you might end up somewhere else!"

The same degree of care and planning should go into the selection of a mate. And while some characteristics may not be of equal importance, we each have "wants" and "deal breakers" that should be part of our personal list. For example, it may be difficult for a vegetarian to marry a hunter or a marathoner to marry a couch potato.

B. A Relationship List to Consider

I was deep in sorrow after a divorce. Being mired in self-pity, I was in no condition to think about what I wanted in a relationship. I could only focus on the pain brought on by the enormous sense of loss. A counselor asked me to write down/journal what I didn't like about my past relationship. That led to an even more difficult assignment: write down what I wanted in the next relationship. I resisted with all my strength. I was in the throes of emotional darkness! Thinking of anything positive seemed impossible and out of the question!

After resisting for weeks, I took out a sheet of paper and completed the assignment on one page. Writing during the dark days turned out to be both therapeutic and profound. I kept the handwritten list intact, without edit or revision. It captured the powerful feelings of the moment, and I thought should be preserved.

At the top of the page, I wrote "What I Want in a Relationship." The list, with its imperfections, followed:

- Best Friend. A friendship (with implicit trust) that's deeper than the one I have with my best friend, my college room-mate.

- Companion. Someone to truly share the ups and downs of the rest of my life.

- Respect and admiration. Who will respect me as a man and admire the things I've done. Will look at me with adoring eyes.

- Challenge me. Will stimulate and challenge me mentally. Intelligent. Has bright eyes!

- Support me. In my job and career. Unconditional support.

- Inspire the children. A positive role model who will nurture and inspire them to be the best they can be – especially my daughter.

- Love me. Love me for who I am (faults and all) and despite my flaws.

- Laugh (sense of humor). A lot of laughter – even (and especially) when stupid things happen. Can she laugh at life's trials, without demeaning or blaming? Can be teased!

- Responsible. But light-hearted (not too serious).

- Protect me. Nurturing. Will not attack me.

- Athletic. Active and enjoys hiking, etc.

- Words of admiration/affirmation. Who uses words to build me up and not tear me down.

- Communication. Listens to understand. Asks me what I want. Sets and respects boundaries. Fights fair (not personal). Forgets quickly.

- Self-confidence and self-esteem. Does not look to others for self-validation or own happiness. Is not self centered or self absorbed.

- Accepts responsibility. Does not blame others.
- Committed to prayer.

Imagine you found a person with some of these characteristics. Imagine, for a moment, life with a companion who was your best friend and who was the type of person that inspired others. I am fortunate to have best friends from grade school, college, law school and a co-worker I met during my first days on the job as a lawyer. These best friends love me unconditionally and despite my faults and failings as a human being (A best friend is someone who knows all the bad stuff about you, but likes you anyway!). They use positive words to build me up. They support me during the tough times and will do anything for me. I confide in them, tell them the awful truth and they don't judge me. They listen to understand and help me to see things clearly. I can ask them a question and they always lead me down the right path. I'm totally secure in their presence and feel safe. Our trust is implicit. Above all, we laugh about all the things that happen to us. We laugh even harder at our silly quarks and habits that, predictably, lead to trouble. Can you imagine the quality and richness of such a relationship with your special someone?

LESSONS LEARNED LATE:

- Would you rent a car in a strange city and drive out of the lot without a map/directions? Never! The same care and thought should be given to identifying the characteristics you want to find in that special mate.
- Make a list. Write down the characteristics that are important to you. You can borrow from mine, if you'd like.
- You are searching for that one best friend, an intimate friend that will be there above all others.
- Like a road map, your list will guide you to the type of person you want.

- If someone violates an important term, treat it as a big warning sign that this person may not be "the one" for you. Make them accountable.

- Make sure you live up to your list.

18. THE WAITING BEGINS: BE THE PERSON YOU WANT TO MEET

You've carefully thought through your "wish list" for that perfect mate. This time, however, you are actually considering which characteristics and interests your special someone must have. You are consciously thinking about the "must haves" on the one hand, and "deal breakers," on the other. You allow your head to do more of the searching for once, rather than letting your heart run wild as you did in the past. After all, that's part of the reason you find yourself where you are today.

Good for you. You're about to experience a time of positive change in a new direction. A time to, once and for all, break the patterns of the past. Upon reflection, you may have been locked in a cycle of behavior that caused you to jump from one unhappy or even toxic relationship to another.

A week goes by. A month and then two. It seems your prince/princess has been delayed in traffic. Stuck somewhere on the highway of life. Don't they just show up on your doorstep? It wasn't supposed to be this way. We live in a world of instant gratification. A TV show runs through a full plot in only one hour. Why isn't this working? OK, I'll give it one more month, and then I'll fall into total despair!

This may be a news flash, but you are not the only person in the universe. There are higher powers at work than you and you are not in charge. While I believe in the power of personal intention, the timing of it is beyond your control. And, for your plan to succeed, there is one more element that must be present.

That element is: You must first be the person you want to meet. That's right – in order for this wonderful person to find you and connect, you must be that person first. You must possess and live the very characteristics that you are looking for. On a sheet of paper, write down the characteristics you desire. Now, go through the list and apply each to yourself. In order for you to find an honest person, you must be honest. If you want "kind, caring and considerate," then you must live those attributes. How do you treat people you don't know, such as sales clerks or wait staff? Are you kind to animals? Do you return your grocery shopping carts? Ouch. Sounds like we all have a lot of work to do.

The time spent waiting becomes a critical time of reflection and introspection. What are your good qualities? What are your "not so good" qualities? What do you need to do to improve your mind, body and spirit? This is a period in which your "goal a day" plan should be kicked into overdrive. You know what the plan looks like. Eat less. Exercise more. Complain less. Be more grateful for the blessings in your life. Be thankful for the little joys of life. Smile. Rediscover and reconnect with your religion. Read self-help books and seek counseling in order to figure out what events in your past have propelled you down the wrong path today. Make new choices that will lead you to be the person you want to meet. The upside: you will feel fabulous and radiate positive energy that will be attractive to everyone with whom you come in contact.

I have another silly theory to share. After a divorce or end of a serious relationship, the natural tendency is to rush into the next one. Rarely is that good for you. It's important to take time to assess what went wrong and how you and your actions contributed to it. It's also a numbers game. You need to meet a lot of people to get a good idea of what you want, what's good for you and what's not. So, my theory is that the first few people you meet immediately after the end of a serious relationship are like waffles. For whatever reason, the first few waffles are never any good. They need to be prepared, only to be thrown away. Beginning with the third, the waffles are good and can be enjoyed!

LESSONS LEARNED LATE:

- Good things take time.
- Rebound relationships are like waffles: the first few are never any good.
- You are neither in charge nor in control.
- Be a victor, not a victim.
- Be the person you want to meet. Be the treasure you want to find.
- List the characteristics and apply them to yourself (this will surely cut your list in half!).
- Time spent waiting can be some of the most productive and dynamic in your lifetime.
- Change starts with one small step in a different direction.
- Unwrap the gifts you've been given. Daily. Alone.
- Love yourself.
- Would you rather be alone and emotionally healthy or stuck in an unhealthy relationship, with perpetual struggles?

19. THIS IS THE ONE (BUT THE WARNING SIGNS ARE FLASHING)!

You've just met a special someone and you're convinced this is "the one." It was love at first sight and you've been together constantly. Cupid shot his arrows and simultaneously hit you both squarely in the heart. You think about this person twenty-four/seven and are overpowered by the "love drug." You want to spend every waking moment together, and when you're apart, your heart aches. You've stopped seeing your friends and cut off contact with the outside world. You don't have time to chat and have little interest in sharing stories with your friends. You are blinded by love. By any measure, your life is perfect, intoxicating, in fact. You're so blissful you could kiss the mailman. If only it could stay this way forever.

While still in the throes of bliss, you notice certain "flaws." Your soul mate may be rude to a sales clerk. She may not be kind to animals. He may display flashes of anger for no apparent reason. She may "cut in line," or insist on being "right." He may be disrespectful or dismissive of your feelings and start to be jealous and controlling. While otherwise calm, his attitude totally changes when he gets behind the wheel, displaying "passive/aggressive" behavior. The warning lights are flashing and the only question is are you paying attention? Are you on the lookout for these familiar warning signs that have appeared in the past? Chances are, your friends have noticed and are there to help you, if you'd only ask. They'd tell you this person does not share your values and "is not good for you." Has this happened to you? Is this the beginning of a country and western song?

There are things that happen in life (repeatedly, it seems) that I can't explain but I know are true. In the context of relationships, I believe it works like this. If you experienced trauma in your childhood (and most of us did), you will have an almost unconscious drive to find relationships that repeat the dysfunction. You will pursue or attract relationships that are not healthy for you. If your father was an alcoholic, you will likely seek out and find that personality in your adult relationships. If you were emotionally abused as a child, chances are you will find that drama replayed again. If you wished someone had "saved" you as a child, you may seek a mate who "needs" to be saved. If your mother and father had a difficult relationship, you are likely inclined to repeat their dysfunctional behavior. Looking back, was your family locked in a cycle of co-dependency? Are you seeing signs of a repeat? Again, I can't explain why this happens and will leave the "cause and effect" analysis to the experts.

I believe that a person's patterns of the past, developed in childhood, will be repeated until that person comes to terms with them. The same relationships, the same patterns of behavior, will be repeated in adulthood, until a person "comes to grips" with the underlying cause and "once and for all" deals with it. There's an elephant in the room, the saying goes, and rather than ignore it (it will never go away), you need to address it head on. Acknowledge the problem, admit it, and resolve to act in a new and different way. When you do, you'll be liberated from the shackles of the past. You'll be rewarded with a wonderful life lived well and a future well lived.

I imagine that we each have a door that leads to a dark room. That room holds our secrets of the past, the ones we want to avoid at all costs. You hold the keys and can open that door anytime you want. But opening the door takes courage and a belief that the pain of dealing with those problems is "worth it." In order to open the door, you must be convinced that there awaits, on the other side, the joy and pleasure of a wonderful new life. When will you open your door? That's hard to predict. Ultimately, you'll do so when the pain of living with these problems is worse than the emotional pain you believe you'll experience when you face your past. When the pain of life is greater than the perceived pain of recovery.

Get busy and put a stop to your dysfunctional relationship cycles of the past. Get help. You don't have to live this way. Buy some self-help books and get started. Find a therapist and make an appointment. Attend "recovery" meetings and discover you are not alone. You have a fabulous life of grace and gratitude waiting for you. You have loved ones who are waiting for your abundant love. You have smiles waiting to be given and received. And when you do find your "healthy" soul mate, you'll be ready to chart a new course for your relationship. Imagine the joy such a "healthy" relationship would bring!

I have one other "sobering" thought to share (pun intended). If you find yourself attracted to others with addictive behaviors (or if you are in such a relationship), a word of caution. I'm no expert and I've not done the research, but I believe a relationship with a mate with addictions is destined to fail for at least three reasons. First, neither of you will understand the other. The person with the addictions is controlled by a higher force, the addictive craving, and is incapable of putting that aside to discuss issues of reason, rationality, truth and accountability. The non-addictive person believes that the other person sees life as they do. This includes the ability to rationally think things through, understand the consequences of ones actions (and the impact those actions have on others) and to change. The non-addictive person believes that, given time, you'll change and life will return to normal. It's simple, just like any other problem in life. In short, there are two people who have diametrically opposed views of the world and their relationship. Second, a life of addiction is exhausting because the object will never satisfy the desire. Each day, an addicted person runs off in the pursuit of something that will always be beyond reach. Third, I don't believe addictions come in "ones." I don't think a person has just one addiction in their personality. This makes dealing with it and overcoming it all the more daunting.

LESSONS LEARNED LATE:

- This is "the one" but your relationship warning lights are flashing.

- Does he/she respect you and share the same values (or not)?

- Is this relationship a repeat of your dysfunctional past?

- Chances are, your friends have noticed and can give you a "reality check." They've seen the cycles of your past.

- Have you acknowledged the "elephant in the room?"

- There's a door that leads to a dark room holding the emotional secrets of your past.

- You hold the key and can open it whenever you want.

- Stop repeating your predictable relationship patterns.

- Get the help you need to open your door and "once and for all" resolve your past.

- Throw the key away.

- Discover the joy of a healthy relationship.

- You have a fabulous life of grace and gratitude waiting for you.

- You have loved ones who are waiting for the joy of your abundant love.

20. THE TWO "MUST HAVE" INGREDIENTS FOR A GREAT RELATIONSHIP

A. Emotional Security

i. Our Happy Tag

No matter how you say it, the foundation of any close relationship is emotional security. If you don't feel safe, the relationship will disintegrate over time. Since this is a basic need borne of our human condition, the euphoric feelings of love might cause you to gloss over it for a time. But eventually a lack of security will prove fatal. Since this is so obvious, how could it ever happen? How is it possible that you would hurt someone you love? How could you make your soul mate feel emotionally "unsafe?"

History, our own experiences and country and western music song titles tell us the answer is "easy." We are each busy sabotaging the very relationships we covet. We do so for at least the following reasons: our selfish interests overpower us and render us incapable of putting the needs of another person first. Most of us, in one way or another, were raised in a dysfunctional childhood environment. And we were never given the instruction manual.

To put it simply, we don't know any better and we let our selfish ego overpower the needs of others. It's like we all have an emotional dragster inside that's ready to roar down the straightaway intently focused on beating the other guy to the finish line. The object, we come to believe, is to finish first, even at the expense of others. There can't be two winners and, just at a point in life when we may be ready to believe otherwise, someone we trusted burns us. Virtually all of our emotional experiences drive home the point that if you're not in control you'll be hurt. It's either "power over" or "power under" and who wants any more pain? The battle lines are inexorably drawn and the fight is on.

So, we have a choice. A choice we must make daily. For lack of a better term, it's to choose happiness. If life came with an instruction manual, one of the first chapters would be on happiness. No doubt, the instruction on happiness would include a large bold warning forced upon us by the lawyers:

WARNING: FAILURE TO FOLLOW THESE HAPPY DIRECTIONS WILL SUBJECT YOU TO A LIFETIME OF MISERY AND EMOTIONAL FAILURE! IF YOU BELIEVE YOU ARE THE FIRST PERSON IN THE HISTORY OF MANKIND TO WHOM THESE RULES DO NOT APPLY, YOUR WARRANTY WILL BE VOID! SIDE EFFECTS INCLUDE, BUT ARE NOT LIMITED TO, DIZZINESS, SADNESS (POSSIBLE DEPRESSION), LONELINESS, FRUSTRATION, DESPAIR, EXHAUSTION AND THE POSSIBILITY OF HAVING A COUNTRY AND WESTERN MUSIC SONG TITLE NAMED AFTER YOUR LIFE! THIS TAG MAY NOT BE REMOVED UNDER PENALTY OF LAW!

Ouch! Would you do something if you knew it would void your warranty? Do you leave the warning tags on your mattress? Of course you do – because there is a label that directs you not to remove them under penalty of law! Like mattresses, we are all born with a tag that says "Certified Happy." Don't you want your happy tag to stay on?

Everything we do and say is a choice. So make a goal: the goal for today will be to make every choice in favor of happiness. It will start with your face: smile. Smile at your spouse (boy, won't that make them wonder what you've been up to!), at your kids (so easy and natural when they're young – and how did that habit get lost as they grew older?), and then continue smiling at everyone you meet. Watch their reaction – a smile is proof that you get back what you give in life. You give a smile and you'll be sure to get one back. What a joy that is. By the way, if you have doubts, catch a baby's attention and smile. You'll be rewarded with a beautiful baby smile in return.

But smiling is easy, you protest! Providing emotional security to another in a relationship looks like a tall mountain to climb with no clearly defined trail to the top. I agree it looks daunting, but change starts with a small step in a new direction. So, make a goal today: I will commit to be the first to offer words and actions that make you feel secure. I will use positive words to build you up. I will earn your emotional trust and when you feel vulnerable, I will respond with loving respect.

Why should I be the first to do this, you ask? Because you want it back. But wait. I'm not perfect! True, and so when (not if), you fall short, apologize. Yes, that's right. Learn to apologize. A good apology goes like this: "I know [insert stupid thing here] bothered you and I'm sorry I did it. I apologize. Will you forgive me? What could I do to make it better?"

After smiling and apologizing, there is something else every couple should do. Write letters, notes and send cards to each other. The written word is powerful times two. A person who writes positive words will be filled with positive thoughts. By writing, thoughts are turned to action. Your stress level will go down and the loving feelings for your spouse/other will be rekindled. In the back of your mind, you might even be reconnecting with the early passion in your relationship. "So, that's why I fell in love with the lug!" Imagine the positive feelings of receiving a "sticky" note on the steering wheel of your car that says, "I love you, honey!" Imagine the warm glow created by a mushy card received in the mail. Above all, imagine the positive, connective benefits of receiving a love letter written for no reason at all.

Ronald Reagan was famous for many accomplishments in his life. Actor, writer, governor, President. What might be less appreciated or understood, was his penchant for writing love letters to his wife, Nancy. As President, with the weight of the world's problems on his shoulders, he had the presence of mind to stop and jot down a "love note" to the love of his life. Imagine the power of that act. Imagine living such a balanced life that it was a priority to stop the other "important" activities and take time out to write a missive. Imagine the love for his wife he rekindled with each note, and the loving warmth and security he created for her when she received such a message. Was there any doubt Nancy was the most important thing in his life?

Writing to a loved one is a powerful act. Today, it can be done through email and text message. Yet, using a pen and paper has the most impact of all.

LESSONS LEARNED LATE:

- The foundation of any close relationship is emotional security.
- Are you busy sabotaging the relationship you covet?
- Is your ego in the way?
- A daily choice: choose happiness.
- Don't you want your "certified happy" tag to stay on?
- Be the first to offer positive words and actions that make others feel secure.
- Apologize.
- "I know [insert stupid thing here] bothered you and I'm sorry. What can I do to make it better?"
- Write love letters.
- Remember the power of the positive word.

ii. Two Questions That Will Guarantee Emotional Security

My objective is to take the many possibilities and reduce them to a few simple action items. A few things you are sure to remember and, if you do them, are sure to produce positive results. With that objective in mind, I'm confident that if you frequently ask your partner two questions, you are certain to have a great and secure relationship.

Do you want emotional security in your relationship? If so, you should frequently ask your partner these two questions:

- What is the one thing I could do for you today that would make you feel better?

- What is the one thing I do that makes you feel emotionally unsafe?

After your partner shares his/her answers, your only response should be "Thank you for sharing your feelings. I'll get started." Then, the process should be repeated, with your partner asking you these questions. To maximize the benefit, your answers should be brief and specific. You'll be amazed at the positive affect these questions will have on your relationship.

B. Learn to Fight

i. Safe to Express Feelings Without Blame

Sounds harsh, doesn't it? You are supposed to learn to fight with your "soul mate." Wait a minute! There must be a mistake!

Truth be told, in that Instruction Manual on Life, another chapter would be devoted to learning how to successfully fight. There are two people in a relationship (for some, this, in itself, may be an awakening) which means conflict is both inevitable and healthy. But, like me making jewelry for Dad, it seems to have failure written all over it. The reasons are predictable. We spend years going to school learning about math and English, but have no course offerings in how to successfully resolve conflict. What we do know we learned by watching and repeating the dysfunctional behavior of others, most likely our parents. Isn't it time to learn a new life skill and give and receive happiness? What if you could learn how to disagree in a loving, respectful manner?

The four words every man hates to hear are: "I'd like to talk." Uh, oh. Whether involuntary or learned, these words instill fear in us. It runs to our core and seems to trigger a "fight or flight" instinct. But the conversation not only needs to, but has to, take place. So, men, get ready. And, ladies, it goes both ways. Communication is a two way street. Men not only need to learn to receive but to say, "Honey, I want to talk," and know they are safe to do so.

There are two objectives that must be reached in order for any communication to be successful. The person speaking must believe they have been (a) listened to and (b) understood. Needing both makes it very difficult. Because, for example, if I start a conversation with harsh words or by blaming you, it will be almost impossible for you to just listen and then patiently wait to convince me that you both listened and understood. Instead, you, the listener on the receiving end, will immediately begin to defend, deflect or change the subject. It's predictable behavior repeated over and over.

Imagine how good your relationship could be if you mastered the art of communication. Imagine if you could communicate with ease, even on the toughest of subjects. Imagine if you could share your honest feelings in a safe and secure environment. Imagine if your first reaction was to disagree with love by showing respect for each other's opinions. Imagine the warmth you'd feel if you knew, no matter the subject, you'd be listened to and understood.

The first challenge is to learn how to start. How do you find a way to start slowly, with love and respect, rather than with harshness (that is guaranteed to end in failure)? Here goes.

Effective conflict resolution (our goal here) must have ground rules. These rules must be understood by both sides and agreed to in advance. A forum must be offered where each side will get time to "state their case" or air their grievances. But it should go further — the speaker must know that she has been both heard and understood. It's not enough for one side to talk while the other party says "yup, yup, yup ..." Understanding leads to contentment (Because the other person can say, for example, Gee, I didn't know squeezing the toothpaste from the middle bothered you) and ultimately to creative problem-solving (I'll buy a spa weekend gift certificate for your mother, so she can stay at the hotel instead of with us!).

This is why mediation is so successful. A mediator is hired to listen to both sides without judging either. He/she must try to find and "carve out" common ground, and then work towards both conventional and creative solutions. Both sides feel understood when asked, essentially, "Now that you've expressed your feelings, what do you want that will make it better?" The conversational journey is completed and each side understands they've both given and received. Each side explained, compromised and got it resolved by laying claim to what they really wanted.

Resistance can be grounded in uncertainty. The key is to create rules that apply to, and can be used by, both. A constitutional lawyer would call this "procedural due process." It's like signing up for perpetual mediation, with a small twist. The twist is, there are two people emotionally entwined who are being asked to master this life skill. This requires some extra help, because the tendency is to "keep score" and get back at the other person when the opportunity arises. Arguing becomes "payback time," or worse.

Good fighting is about being able to express feelings without blame. It's about saying "I felt bad when you did this and I want you to understand it bothered me and why it's important to me." The other person responds in a loving, respectful way by saying "Thank you for sharing your feelings."

It sounds easy and makes common sense. However, when tensions rise between a couple, it is extremely difficult to start a calm and reflective discussion. Additional help is needed, especially in the "how to start" department. American Indian tribes believed that every member should have a voice. To accomplish this goal, they would gather everyone in a circle and let them talk in turn. To insure order and respect, they used the "talking stick." If you held the talking stick, two things happened: you were the only one who could talk and everyone else had to listen. No lawyerly interruptions or rebuttals. No arguing "yes, buts."

ii. Six Steps For a Successful Fight

Here are the six steps for a successful fight:

STEP ONE: To start the difficult conversation, say, "I'd like to have the talking stick." This signals that the conversation is important and needs to occur. No backing out.

STEP TWO: The other person responds either yes, let's do it now (and I'll stop what I'm doing) or proposes a specific time for the discussion (within hours, not days or weeks!). There are admittedly bad times to talk and a better time can/should be set.

STEP THREE: Only the person with the talking stick can talk. The conversation belongs to them.

STEP FOUR: The person with the talking stick says:

"I feel [name the feeling ... bad, sad, insecure, hurt]

About [describe stupid thing done by the other person]

Because [explain why it bothers you]

STEP FIVE: The other person repeats the message. "So, what I heard you say is ..., correct? The message gets repeated until the person with the talking stick confirms that yes, the message was received and understood.

STEP SIX: The other person says: "Thank you for sharing your feelings."

In order for any conversation to be meaningful and, therefore, successful, the person talking must walk away believing they were listened to and the message was understood. Using the talking stick, whether actual or just a metaphor, puts both parties on notice of the rules of engagement. Both know how it will start and how it will end. This, in itself, is of enormous value. It accomplishes another goal as well – preventing a harsh start up. If you have the talking stick, you can't blame and make it personal. Your words must describe how you feel about some event and explain why it matters to you. Your feelings are legitimate and, besides, it's probably how we handle a disagreement at work between co-workers or with clients. We're not fully aware we have these communication skills and simply need to bring them home to our loved ones.

Communication is a two way street: things go both ways and apply equally. If you walk up the street (with the talking stick in hand), you must be equally adept at walking back "with your listening ears on." So, when the conversation is over and concluded, the other person can ask for the talking stick. Then, the entire six steps are repeated with the roles reversed.

LESSONS LEARNED LATE:

- Imagine if you could communicate with ease, even on the most sensitive subjects.

- Effective communication requires that the speaker be listened to and understood.

- No argument has ever been won.

- Start a difficult conversation, with "I'd like the talking stick."

- Follow the six easy steps. Practice them together and take turns with "the stick."

- Do you have your listening ears on?

- Celebrate your progress with dinner and a movie/something fun.

21. WHAT YOU FIGHT ABOUT IS NOT WHAT YOU'RE FIGHTING ABOUT

Now that you've agreed on the method or "procedure" for fighting, what do couples fight about? Even if you're both good at explaining and being understood, will anything ever get resolved? Or will you simply be locked in perpetual battle, albeit at a lower decibel level? The reality is that what you fight about at the moment is not what you're really fighting about. It's much deeper. It is rooted in unspoken meaning, fears and experiences of the past. It's why couples get locked in perpetual arguments, replayed over and over. What if you could find understanding and break through to a life of harmony?

I'm no expert, that's for sure. Whenever I tackle a tough subject, I try to divide the universe of possibilities into "threes." There's no magic or science to this. It's readily apparent that reality can never be neatly divided into "three" of anything. But a group of "three" simplifies the complexity into manageable portions. I can understand three things and remember them for future reference. On balance, it seems like the benefits outweigh the shortcomings of my system, so I'll proceed with my three categories.

I believe there are three categories of things couples argue over/about, and perpetually so:

- Little things that can easily be changed by the one doing them, or just as easily ignored by the one bothered.

- Medium things that can't be changed. If you argue over these, you will be locked in a perpetual downward spiral. But if you objectively step back, these issues can never be resolved and therefore must be understood as "facts of life" and managed appropriately by the couple. Most often, the one farthest removed from the issue, must "let it go."

And the one closest must come to the other's rescue/defense.

- Big things that represent the proverbial elephant in the room. They are extremely difficult and complex. They have both objective appearance and subjective/hidden meaning that will vary wildly from person to person. These issues must be successfully dealt with and resolved by both parties.

A. The Little Things: Some Changed, Most Ignored

When you are in love, you see only the good things. Your "soul mate" has no flaws, only cute little "quirky" things they do that seem endearing. After the bloom of love wears off, "yuck" what awful habits you have! Were you raised by wolves in the wilderness? How long have you picked your teeth like that, and in public no less! The truth is, we each have crazy/silly little habits that over time are sure to drive others to distraction. Some of these can be changed, if we were aware that they really mattered to our soul mate. But most can't be changed. Our little habits make up who we are as individuals and are part of our "uniqueness."

If you insist that the other person change, remember this: You can change tires, but not people. But wait! Change in all things is possible, you protest! Ok, let's assume you really want the other person to change. If so, your request is legitimate only on one condition: you change first. Now, assuming you've resolved in your own mind that you will offer to change first, my advice is to turn it into a game. That's right, make it fun. Here's a little secret – men like games and will be more willing to "go there" if it's wrapped in something that looks like a game.

Game 1: Swap and Drop

Hold a list-swapping event at a specific time. In preparation, each person makes a small list (no more than five to ten) of the things the other person does that drives them crazy, and then exchange lists. The exchange must occur at the same time and on the same terms. That is, each understands this is a "free" chance to make a list and each agrees, in advance, to pick some things on the list given to them to work on and change (not more than three). The list must be small and the items specific. The items must be capable of being changed and not personality traits, for example. The things a person agrees to change must be circled/checked, so there is accountability. Make sure there's lots of laughter and the more it looks like a game, the better.

Game 2: Turnabout is Fair Play

Each person makes a list of five things the other person does that drives them crazy and then the couple exchanges lists. After revealing their list to each other, the lists are returned. Then, each person selects something on his or her list that the other person does and for one day engages in "turnabout." That is, with full knowledge, they each adopt one "bad" habit of the other. So, if Husband leaves his clothes on the floor and Wife is always late (just a made-up example, no doubt!), they agree to "reverse roles" for a day to see what it's like. Walking in another person's shoes is a great way to learn. It won't take long before the other person "sees" how their behavior "looks" and quickly realizes it might be a good idea to change.

To earn "bonus" points, give yourself a reward at the end of the game. Treat yourself to a nice dinner or maybe a hike/bike on a trail. Games should offer a fun ending and lots of laughter. You can smile knowing you've grown as a couple and put the "little" things in their proper place.

For the rest of the little things: get over it and move on. Look at these little things as endearing qualities that make him/her unique. Laugh with and at the little things. Why? Because we are all perfectly imperfect. None of us can claim the "I'm better than you" mantle. So, choose happiness and decide there's an ever-increasing list of things that don't matter. Then work diligently to expand the list.

Then, laugh. You will be rewarded with a happy heart, and a content mate. Besides, it's no fun to be criticized. Isn't that one of the lessons we learned as a kid on the playground?

Hey, Buster, you say! Telling someone to "just get over it" is not very helpful and only proves I've got a firm grasp of the obvious. How about some help! In the fields of engineering and construction, the term "workaround" is often used to describe a way to "fix" an intractable problem. Instead of fixing the source of the problem, which might take too much time or money, you literally "work-around" it and find other alternatives. How might this concept be applied to problem spots in a relationship? Let's assume one person is punctual and one perpetually runs late. If the "runs late" person calls and says "I'm getting ready to leave my office and catch a cab to meet you at the restaurant," the punctual one will immediately take action, catch a cab and arrive five minutes early at the restaurant. This is what punctual people do as a matter of habit. However, the "perpetually late" person has habits too, which cause him to always run a few minutes behind. He had to "wrap things up," return one last call and tell the staff to have a great weekend. The predictable result: the "on time" person is sitting at the restaurant mad and frustrated. Is this the way to start a great evening together?

To deal with these "little" and predictable problems, put your mind to work and create a "workaround" solution. If the scenario above is your situation, perhaps you could ask him to "call back" when he actually walks out and reaches the street. The later in the sequence of events you can get him to call, the more "in sync" your timing will be.

Consider the situation when a woman asks a man to shower and get ready. Men are task oriented and will generally hop up, shave, take a shower and be dressed in about 9 minutes. It doesn't take most men that long to get ready (and there's no question, we have a lot less to do to accomplish the task). Now what? Typically, the man will be waiting and will get frustrated. A "skirmish" will no doubt break out and the evening will be off to a rotten start. What to do to avoid this "no win" proposition? The man, in my example, should shower, dress and get out of the way. Then, have a plan to read a book or do some other task while you're waiting. Make productive use of your free time! One guy told me this plan worked so well that, recently, he waited so long, he almost finished his personal tax return! Well done!

LESSONS LEARNED LATE:

- You can change tires, but not people.
- Resolve that you will change first.
- Turn the change process into a game. Make it fun.
- Start with "swap and drop," and "turnabout is fair play."
- Instead of fixing the other person, create your own "work-around" solution.
- Create an ever-expanding list of things that don't matter.
- Laugh and you'll be rewarded with a happy heart.

B. The Medium Things: Irreconcilable and Unsolvable

There are certain facts that are not going to change. Our crazy family members (I'm convinced, no one is immune from this fact of life) and the nonsensical things they say. A person's relationship with their parents which is a complex mosaic (chances are, dysfunctional in some way). A person's religion, ethnicity, upbringing, physical features and even the things they are passionate about, ranging from hobbies to teams they cheer for (a constant since they were a kid). I'm sure you can think of many more. These "facts of life" are basically the cards you're dealt. Whatever they are, they are and there's nothing you or anyone else can do to change them. So, arguing over and over about things that can't be changed is futile. It can't help and can only hurt. The more you lock horns on these issues, the more resentment builds. It's a downward spiral – a race to the bottom.

The sooner that a couple can identify these unsolvable issues and put them in their proper place, the better off they will be. Be on the lookout for these issues and put them aside. Your happiness is at stake and nothing should get in the way of the enjoyment of your partner. You will never reach your potential as a couple if these issues "bubble up" as points of contention in times of stress. It's an obvious "no win."

There is one caveat, however. Especially when dealing with family, there is a point in time that the son/daughter must rise up to defend his/her partner. While you can't change others, you don't need to stand there and take it. In fact, one of the most powerful acts of love you can show your spouse is to make it clear that if the family wants a choice, you are choosing the happiness/integrity of your partner. You are married now, and your allegiance is owed to your mate. You can figure out a diplomatic way to say it, but the bottom line is that you must choose to protect and honor your spouse. There's no middle ground and it will take courage. On the other hand, the positive impact on your marriage will be lasting and profound.

LESSONS LEARNED LATE:

- A person's "facts of life" are not going to change.
- Ideas can evolve, but beliefs are hard to change.
- Arguing over things that can't be changed is futile.
- Identify unsolvable issues and put them aside.
- Choose acceptance over resentment.
- Respect the other person.
- At some point, you must choose to protect and honor your spouse.

C. The Big Things Must Be Discussed and Resolved

The big things are the issues that loom large and cannot be ignored. Like a peace treaty between countries, they must be "placed on the table" and negotiated to the satisfaction of both parties. Each side will initially insist on their own way and will be suspicious of the other. Gradually, with patience and understanding, the two sides will become untethered from their moorings and move towards compromise. It will take the skills of a diplomat, but the essence of the relationship is at stake.

What are they? I can think of at least three: Money, sex and raising children. There's good news here. Any discussion of sex would require another book that I'm not going to write, and, if I did, it would be filled with blank, white pages interrupted with a few words like "huh," "do what?" and "do we have to talk about this now?" Happily, I will leave that topic for you intelligent readers to figure out. I will briefly tackle the subject of money. The subject of raising children is a lengthy one and is discussed in detail in Part III.

i. Money

The subject of money seems to be toxic. It's so difficult to deal with because it has both an objective and subjective or hidden meaning. Each partner could have been raised in the same type of environment, yet form a completely different opinion about what money means to them and how to manage it. Each partner could have grown up with no money as a child, yet one will be a serious saver (because she had none) and the other a spender (because he had none). One can only sleep at night with money in the bank and the other only if there's something to spend. The same childhood experience can lead to opposite values and behavior as an adult. Money also represents power and is sure to be a source of struggle for control. Sounds like the worst of circumstances and a source of endless battle.

A business has short-term operating expenses and long-term or "capital" expenditures. The day-to-day bills are set and must be paid.

The amount must be matched with sufficient cash flow. These items are predictable and can be listed and agreed on. If there's "negative" cash flow, then the business must immediately put a plan in place to reduce costs and increase revenue. A "cost cutting" plan is agreed upon and spending is reduced. The process is painful, but everyone is on board and understands the urgency of the situation.

The long-term expenditures are really the product of a dream of where the business ought to be going. It's the result of long-term planning, based on a shared agreement of future plans/goals/objectives and what it will take to get there. Businesses manage this process with "goal setting" meetings. The options (dreams, really) are put on the table, fully vetted, and then a consensus is reached on what the long-term goals are and how much it will cost to achieve them. The amount of money needed is carefully determined and then plans are put in place to save or "reserve" cash from current earnings or borrow additional amounts from a lender.

So it is with a couple managing their finances. A household is a "business" with revenue and expenses. There are the monthly bills to be paid (representing past decisions made) and the long-term dreams or ambitions of where the couple wants to be in the future. Maybe it is this simple, but reality has a way of proving us wrong.

Here are some ideas for you to consider. Both partners need to be involved in the short term bill paying, so that each understands where the money is going on a monthly basis (and can't run around saying "where's all the money gone!"). They must agree on a budget and then each be accountable. However, I'm convinced a person needs some independence and some of their own money to spend as they wish. Whether it's called an "allowance" or "spending money" there must be an amount set aside for each that can be spent in whatever way that person decides. No asking permission, no comments please.

The couple must also have a long-term financial plan they've discussed. A business must engage in long-term "goal setting" (and won't survive without one). A couple must do the same. However, these goals also represent the dreams realized and, therefore, care must be taken to allow each person to express their hopes/fears/dreams and ambitions. If one dreams of a cabin in the woods (translated: spending), while the other dreams of early retirement (translated: saving), each dream must be expressed and validated. Then a plan put in place to reach them. Why? Because there's no choice. As responsible adults, you must work together to manage your money.

ii. My Assistant's Proven Money Short-cut

I explained my theories on money management to my long-time assistant. She nodded in approval (you could say she's good at "yupping" the boss!). I asked her what she thought. She really liked my ideas. We engaged in some great discussion and I made some changes based on her input. Then, I asked her how she and her new husband handle the subject of money. Her answer: "Easy. We keep separate checkbooks – and then when I run out of money, I just ask him for more!"

LESSONS LEARNED LATE:

- What does money represent in your life?
- Are you a spender or a saver?
- Are you prepared to set a budget and be accountable?
- While managing together, each person must have their own money to spend as they wish.
- Have you agreed on long-term financial goals?
- Take my assistant's advice: keep separate checkbooks and when you run out, ask for more!

22. GETTING TO KNOW YOU: THE POWER OF PERSONALITY

How well do your know your companion? Do you know all of her hopes and dreams and where they came from? Do you understand what her dreams represent? Have you fully explored her personality type and how she responds in good times and bad? Do you know her fears and how they were created? Has she shared her childhood experiences and how they've shaped her adult life?

Most likely, you've been too busy being hopelessly in love to focus on anything else. But the studies show that the euphoric feelings of love wear off anywhere between six months and two years. Without the "love drug" what will sustain you as a couple going forward? As if to make things more difficult, we each are the product of our own environment and see the world through our own lenses. Thus, our tendency is to interact in our own way (the only one we know), and it probably won't connect with the needs or views of the other. The more we try, the more we fail to connect on the other's level and the more frustrated we become. The downward spiral has begun. What can we do to turn this bit of inevitability around?

The best answer is to use every effort to get to know and truly understand your mate. She's a unique one-of-a-kind creation and you must acknowledge it, embrace it, and then put on your detective hat to uncover her history. Your job is to search for family history, childhood experiences and simple likes and dislikes. The differences between you are there, waiting to be uncovered and the sooner you can start the task, the better your relationship will be. If you don't, you could be facing an unending supply of relationship miscues. For example, you have warm memories of the puppy you received as a kid and you want to share that joy with your new companion. Being the romantic devil that you are (no time to underplay your considerable romantic skills!), you find the perfect large breed dog and plan to give the dog to her on her birthday. No doubt, she'll be wowed by your act of love. Except, there's only one problem. While you were running with big dogs as a kid, she was attacked and bitten by one as a little girl. Unbeknownst to you, she is terrified of dogs, and understandably so. A relationship train wreck waiting to happen. Given time, and more pages, it would be easy to create more "nightmare" scenarios. Substitute a cat and find out she has severe allergies. Give her a goldfish and she'll cry at the childhood memory of finding Goldie upside down in the fish tank!

Here are three different sources and approaches to use in "discovering" the personality of your mate. There are many others and I encourage you to find other books on the subject. Some also have practical workbooks, the completion of which can be insightful. Since it's unlikely that you understand your own personality on a deeper level (why do I do the things I do?), you should be equally curious at exploring your own personality traits.

A. Love Language

In his book The Five Love Languages, Gary Chapman writes that we each have unique emotional needs, which, if met, will cause us to become more deeply connected to our loved ones. He concludes that, as our emotional "love tanks" become filled, the quality of our emotional life, our connectedness, increases. While we each have a "love tank," there are five different "love languages" that will cause ours to be filled. Most often, one person will "communicate" in his or her own love language and, unless the other person has the same one, the connection won't be made and the love tank will remain low. This can be overcome, and happiness and connectedness restored, if each person knows what the other's love language is.

The five love languages are words of affirmation, quality time, receiving gifts, acts of service and physical touch. It is easy to understand that, if you are a gift giver and your spouse values quality time, your efforts to communicate in your valued currency, gifts, will have no affect on the love tank of your spouse who craves spending quality time together. This is an easy book to read together and you'll enjoy the process of discovery. Until you both unlock this mystery, your relationship will be filled with frustration, misunderstanding and low love tanks. On the other hand, your marriage is sure to take a great leap forward towards long-lasting love, if you communicate using your mate's love language. Staying connected can be as easy as "checking in" and asking "What's the level of your love tank and what can I do to help fill it up?"

B. Birth Order

Another book that unlocks the mystery of "why you are the way you are," is The Birth Order Book, by Kevin Leman. Dr. Leman believes that a person's personality has been shaped by their upbringing, principally based on a person's birth order. A first-born is a conscientious, reliable, perfectionist who is a natural leader, a serious, logical person who doesn't like surprises. A middle child tends to be a mediating diplomat who avoids conflict, is loyal, independent, secretive, and can be a maverick. The last-born is a charming manipulator who seeks attention, is a people person, a natural salesman, tenacious and loves surprises. An only child was a little adult by age seven, thorough, high achiever, cautious, can't bear to fail and has high expectations for self.

Based on your mate's birth order, you can identify her personality traits. The book then goes into detail about how these traits play out in a relationship and at work. It is both interesting and profound to think that our birth order environment has such a powerful impact on who we become as adults. The book is filled with research data about the birth order of CEO's and astronauts (first born), entrepreneurs (middles or down the order) and salesman or comedians (youngest). A good book to read together and explains how and why each of your children is different.

C. Enneagram Personality Profile

A "deeper dive" in the task of profiling personalities, The Essential Enneagram, is a guide into how you think, what you feel and how

THINGS I WISH I KNEW

you experience life. After answering a series of questions, you are identified with nine personality types, which are perfectionist, giver, performer, romantic, observer, loyal skeptic, epicure and protector. Each of the nine has a "basic proposition," and "principal characteristics." You are then asked to review the personality types and confirm that the description is indeed, you. Obviously, this depth of analysis can be done only on an individual basis. It is especially eye opening because it considers the personality traits that inhibit your growth as a person and then serves as a guide to overcoming them. It also shows how the various types interact, with some being more favorable "couples" and other combinations being more difficult.

LESSONS LEARNED LATE:

- How well, and deeply, do you understand your mate?
- Put on your detective hat to learn about your mate's personality, childhood and background.
- Our personality traits explain how we think, how we feel, what we fear and how we react in good times and bad.
- Learn about your spouse's "love language" and increase your connectedness.
- Using birth order, find and identify your mate's personality traits.
- The Enneagram provides a remarkable "deep dive" into the nine different personality types and how they interact.
- Best friends understand, accept and "just get" each other at the deepest level.
- Best friends have no ego in the game.

23. TRY THIS SECRET TECHNIQUE: ASK FOR WHAT YOU WANT

It must be a secret technique. It could be the headline on one of those tabloid magazines I find myself reading in the grocery store checkout line (hey, I'll admit it!). "Secret Technique Will Get You Everything You Want!" the headline would scream. The byline found inside would say, "Millions of married couples report happiness increased by 43 percent." What am I referring to? The ability to ask, using the simplest words possible, for exactly what you want. It seems most of us must be incapable of this. I know I was. I either couldn't or wouldn't just ask for what I wanted. I would be upset that others didn't guess what I wanted and just do it. After all, the other person knew me well enough and I sure was good at hinting. When I didn't get what I was dreaming about, I'd get frustrated and then resentful over time. Then I'd become resistant and refuse to do things I knew the other person wanted. Sounds ridiculous, doesn't it?

Please try this with your significant other. In the clearest voice, using the simplest words, ask for what you want. Don't hint and don't assume. Don't make the other person be a mind reader. If it's so important to you, ask for exactly what you want. Then, when your significant other asks you for something, but she's unclear, ask her if she means (repeat her request) or tell her you'd like to do what she wants but you're unclear what her request is. Get this right, and your relationship will immediately rocket up to a new level. A level filled with simplicity and clarity and at least 43 percent more happiness (OK, so I made this last part up!).

LESSONS LEARNED LATE:

- Secret Technique Will Get You Everything You Want!
- The Secret: Ask for what you want.
- Use simple words. Be specific.
- I don't know any mind readers. Do you?
- Don't hint. Don't assume.
- Get this right, and your happiness will soar.

24. GOALS, REALITY AND DREAMS OF A LOVE AFFAIR

A. Relationship Goals (An Annual Assessment)

You found your soul mate. Your relationship has been pretty good. You have differences of opinion, but the talking stick has worked. You are each able to share feelings and express opinions without blame, but the relationship just doesn't' seem to be going anywhere. "Stuck in a rut" seems to be a good metaphor for the past year. Don't be surprised, it happens to everyone. After some period of time, a couple will find they are in a routine and the spark is gone. No new topics to discuss (the weather's been fine for months) and no recent problems to overcome.

I'll apologize in advance for borrowing some business practices and applying them to your soul mate, but after a certain period of time, anything in life gets stale. It's the "same old, same old" repeated over time. Good business people know this to be true and fear it as an enemy of a successfully run business. From fear, springs action. The action a business takes is to do an annual assessment and engage in goal setting for the next year. Carefully reviewing the results of last year, the managers decide what worked and should be continued and what didn't and should be changed. This makes eminent sense. If a business continues with a strategy that's not working, it will fail over time. If you were in charge of the business, you wouldn't stick with a "doomed to fail" strategy or business plan, would you? Of course not!

Couples are no different. They should sit down at least once a year and review their relationship plan. Write down what's working and, more importantly, what's not. Then, after each person has had a chance to write down what is and is not working for them, they should meet (just as business managers do), review the other person's list and then decide what should be changed. As important, the couple should set new goals for the year. It can be as simple as this: what are our two or three couple goals for us this year? What steps are we going to take to get better and grow as a couple? It might be to take a child parenting class together. It might be to go on a church marriage retreat for a weekend. It might be to seek "preventive" counseling to learn how to treat each other better or solve an intractable problem. If only one of these steps is taken each year, won't your relationship be better off? Stated differently, you take your car in for preventive maintenance or a tune-up, so why don't you treat your marriage/relationship at least as well as your car?

LESSONS LEARNED LATE:

- Is your relationship "stuck in a rut?"
- Don't wait for the other person, pull yourself out first. Lead by example.
- Each person should make a list (two or three items) of what's working and what's not.
- At least once a year, write down two or three relationship goals and agree on them.
- Make "preventive maintenance" a priority in your relationship.
- Each year, resolve to "get better" and improve as a couple. Take (at least) a class a year.
- Treat your marriage/relationship better than you treat your car!

B. Some Bad News

Since a relationship, by definition, involves two human beings, it is a certainty there will be many times when the individuals are not at the same "emotional place" at any particular moment in time. This must be understood and accepted. There are times of great growth as a couple and then many flat plateaus. There will also be the inevitable times of emotional distance when each feels little connection and wonders how they can even continue as a couple. Fortunately, for most couples, these dark times pass and the better times return. All of life is a cycle, and a relationship is no exception. The mistake is expecting it to be otherwise.

So, here's the bad news. The quality (or lack thereof) of your relationship will be determined by the one who cares the least. Unfortunately, the quality of your relationship will drift downward towards the person least committed, least motivated, or least able to fully engage. So, while one person may be reading the books and be truly motivated to change for the better, the relationship will tend to be stuck with the one at the "lower level."

So, other than giving up or giving in, is there anything that can be done? Yes, there is. Change yourself and act your way up to being a better person. Set a positive tone and model the behavior you want to see. Be candid and say, "I can't change you, but I can sure change me. I'm not happy where I am, emotionally speaking, and I'm going to do something about it." Then, go about proving it and "acting up" to better conduct instead of "acting out." Buy some self-help relationship books and read them. When finished, leave them on your partner's nightstand as a reminder of unfinished business (unfortunately, nagging them to read will only increase their resistance).

A final piece of bad news. It takes two to agree to get married, but only one to get divorced. It takes two "soul mates" to find each other, spend hours, days and months in blissful courtship, and then have a fabulous wedding. It only takes one, however, to drive it into the ditch. One partner can unilaterally decide, "It's over" and then follow through and make it a reality. I wish it weren't true, but the divorce statistics say otherwise. I'm sorry to say it, but this may be a reality you will face.

LESSONS LEARNED LATE:

- Every relationship experiences tough times. The mistake is to think otherwise.

- The person who cares the least will determine the quality of your relationship.

- I can't change you, but I can change me.

- Your decisions reflect your priorities.

- Act up to better conduct instead of "acting out."

- It takes two to get married, but only one to get divorced. I wish it weren't true, but the divorce statistics say otherwise.

C. Imagine a Love Affair With Your Best Friend

I want to leave each topic with an expression of hope for dreams to be realized. Imagine you have a love affair with your very best friend. What would that look like? What would be some of the elements? Since the affair is with your best friend, I know what that looks like and I'm sure you do too. My best friend is the one person I run to when things are good or when things are bad. I want to run to her with my exciting news of the day and I know she'll be my biggest fan. She'll be an unconditional supporter, and she'll acknowledge how hard I've worked, how much I've sacrificed and how proud she is of me. When things go wrong, she'll be in my corner acting as my safety net. She'll want to hear about how bad it was and then, without judgment, sooth my wounded soul. Sometimes she'll try to help me think through my options, but often listening will be enough.

She'll hold me and tell me it'll be all right and I'll believe her. I can tell her anything and I'll be safe, today and forever in the future. She knows the real me, faults and all, better than anyone else. Most of all, we laugh together. We laugh about the things that happen and about how silly we are. We laugh at life, daily, even when it's probably not a laughing matter. As for the love affair, she'll love me more as we age gracefully together. She'll adore me, and express her adoration to me and anyone else who will listen. She'll see beauty in my wrinkles and she'll glow when she speaks of the time when we first met.

I hope you either find or have that love affair with your very best friend. If you don't have it at the moment, I hope you work with all your heart to make it so. Talk with your special someone and share your dreams and aspirations for your relationship. Set the bar high. Then demonstrate your commitment by living up to your fifty percent of the dream. Be that magnificent friend that anyone would be lucky to have. Be the treasure you want to find. Live a life that has, as it's center, a love affair with your best friend.

PART III:
RAISING CHILDREN

25. WHAT KIND OF ADULT DO YOU WANT YOUR CHILD TO BE?

You've found a career and pursued it with a passion. You have a great job. Leading with your head, and not your heart, you found that perfect special someone. You are in the early years of a love affair with your best friend. Congratulations! You've come a long way and are well on your way to leading an extraordinary life. A life of passion lived well. A life with two-thirds of the events completed. Now, it's time to turn your considerable attention to that final frontier: the subject of having kids.

One of the skills of a good lawyer is the ability to look forward in time and imagine the outcome. When the case or project is over, she will ask, what is a great outcome. If you could have any result, what would it look like? Then, after carefully imagining a great result, she will work backwards to identify the steps necessary to obtain that outcome. The lawyer will also consider the variables along the way and try to factor those in as well. Only after this process is complete, will the lawyer return to the starting point and then develop a step-by-step strategy for "winning" the case or successfully completing the business deal or project. I believe there's great value in applying the same "look forward" in deciding how to raise children.

Here's an important question for you to consider. Imagine your baby just turned nineteen. What do you want him to be like? What are his values, attributes, characteristics and level of responsibility? Let's try to come up with a simple list of "must haves" and "don't wants." Despite different backgrounds, etc., I suspect the lists of most parents will look the same.

I want my son/daughter to be kind and respectful, with high self esteem; an independent thinking self starter; high morals and values; comfortable in social settings, interesting to talk to and interested in what others have to say; tolerant of differences; financially responsible, with an understanding of the difference between "needs" and "wants;" able to handle adversity and "bounce back;" and fully ready to live on their own as a functioning adult. On the other hand, I don't want my son/daughter to be mean-spirited and disrespectful, have low self esteem, be selfish or narcissistic and feel entitled; be dependent on others in order to function; have low morals; be intolerant; be financially irresponsible and incapable of living alone. What part of the scouting creed did I leave out?

Is there a place where children with these "good" attributes are raised? I believe there is. Have you met a kid raised on a farm or agricultural environment, especially one raised around animals? A kid raised with chores and age-appropriate responsibilities that grew up making decisions and either enjoying or suffering the consequences. A kid who learned at a young age how to wash his own clothes, cook a healthy meal and set his own alarm clock. A kid who had animals that depended on him for food and water? One who had a job at an early age and had to save his own money to buy the "extras" in life? One who had to wait for the bus (and if he missed the bus, he missed school) competed in athletics (sometimes unsuccessfully) and in county fairs? Can you imagine the positive characteristics of a child raised in this environment?

My simple theme for raising children is to consider the farm example. At the earliest age, give them choices with consequences. The choices are clear and simple and the consequences flow naturally and immediately from the choice. The child's behavior is rewarded with self-esteem building words of affirmation, and disciplined with clear, swift and age appropriate consequences. Then, start to give them responsibility in age-appropriate doses.

At about age 8, give them an allowance equal to their age. They must save their money to buy "extras" and pay for things the child breaks. The child's own money becomes a powerful force in their life and you'll be amazed at the impact on their decision-making. Give them animals to take care of and other important responsibilities. When they're ready, start them cooking and doing chores.

Soon, they can learn to wash their own clothes. Do you see what's happening? Do you see the incredible building blocks being put in place? Can you imagine the qualities of your own farm kid?

I'm no expert in child psychology or on the subject of early childhood development. There are many great books on these subjects written by experts which you can and should read. You also should attend parenting classes and rely on family and friends for advice. Nope, I don't have the expertise, but I'm from Nebraska and I've met a lot of kids raised on a farm. I also spent my formative years working as a laborer on the construction crew and learned the lessons available to those on the business end of a shovel.

Finally, I'd like to digress a moment and pause to ask a question. I've discovered there was, unbeknownst to me, only one reason to go to law school. To learn the skills necessary to stay one step ahead of the three little lawyers I've apparently been raising. Do all kids start out with the characteristics and arguing skills of little lawyers, only to divert to all the other non-lawyer careers when they get older? If you could help me answer this question, I would greatly appreciate it!

LESSONS LEARNED LATE:

- Have you thought deeply about the type of person you want your child to be?
- What are the characteristics of a great nineteen-year-old?
- What are her values, attributes and level of responsibility?
- Consider the attributes of a kid raised on a farm.
- Make a list of "must haves," and "don't wants."
- What steps/actions will you take to create/mold these attributes?
- Are you prepared to stand back and watch as your child tries and fails?

26. HEY BABY!

After a long search, you finally found your soul mate. After a whirlwind courtship, you got engaged. The romance was intoxicating. The other person could do no wrong. There were no fights, just respectful disagreements that were easily resolved because love brought you effortlessly to a place of compromise. The wonderful, magical, dream-of-a-lifetime wedding followed. Then there was the blissful honeymoon to either the sun-drenched beaches of Hawaii (or insert your beach destination here), or the exotic, and utterly hopeless, romance that is the City of Lights, Paris (or insert your romantic city here).

What next? Children, of course! The word "baby" becomes top of mind. Planning, then pregnancy begins and the nesting starts with a determined fury. While the husband is worried about the playoffs, the expectant mother is focused on finishing the nursery, in perfect pastels. Crib rolled in. Changing table ready. Nursing chair stationed at an angle. "Onesies" stacked neatly in the top drawer.

The time leading up to the birth of the first child is uniquely special. Children are God's gift, and the sense of excitement and anticipation can't be explained – only shared. You are experiencing the miracle of life, with the mother experiencing it in painful by painful moment. The father is a witness to bringing a new life into this world. Nothing can be more awe-inspiring. After my sister was born, Dad was so excited when he left the hospital, that he backed his new car over a fire hydrant. His elation was only slightly tempered by his carelessness and the cost of car repair.

Eventually, you bring the little bundle of joy home. After about an hour or so, after the excitement starts to subside, reality sets in. Wait a minute. Only a few hours earlier, highly trained nurses were caring for the newborn infant. They knew what to do. They folded the tiny blanket perfectly around the baby to keep her feeling safe and secure. They knew what the baby needed, when the baby needed it. They could change a diaper with their eyes closed! Now, only a few hours later, this baby depends on her parents for everything. Her very life hangs in the balance, with total and complete dependence on your knowledge and actions. Knowing that someone else's life literally is in your hands is one of the most sobering thoughts possible. Shaken and inspired by reality, you jump to action. How do you fold that tiny blanket so it stays tightly tucked? Does the right flap go under or over ... Uh oh!

I'm certainly less knowledgeable about babies than I am about the other subjects in this book. What I have is not expertise or research to report, but the experience of lessons learned late. I have three younger children so the baby experience is relatively fresh in my mind. I had children later in life. Being an "older" dad had many advantages. After living childless through my twenties and thirties, I'd had a chance to fully focus on my career and spend time alone. Most of my friends had children in their twenties, so I experienced the joy, trials and tribulations of raising a family vicariously through them. Fortunately, I had some great "dad friends" who were wonderful role models for me. Now, it was my turn. I wanted children desperately and was as ready as a man could be for the joy and challenges of having a baby times three. Only after my first child was born did Dad tell me "I couldn't imagine a life without children." He was seventy-eight when he spoke those words. He had kept them hidden from me for forty years.

From the moment of conception, culminating with the moment of birth, your life has inexorably changed. Whatever your experience with love, you will find a new dimension of love that you never knew before. It's different, more profound, and more awe-inspiring. Simply, you've never loved, and never been capable of loving, anything more than a baby. To say its life changing is really an understatement. Of course, that means the challenges facing a couple are more difficult than ever. But with great challenges come great rewards – and there's no greater reward than raising your own child. So, start by loving, loving, loving. Love your baby, love your spouse and love yourself. Feel and revel in the profound growth of your soul. Then, repeat this over and over:"It's not about you!" The more you under-stand "it's not about you," the more your jealous ego will be freed and the better you'll be equipped for the task at hand.

My advice for dads is the advice given to me by my "dad friends" – commit that, for the first year of your baby's life, the baby and her mother will be your top priority.You know what these words mean and you know the level of commitment it takes. You've done this before, whether in athletics, school or at work.You've run up some tall mountains and enjoyed the view from the top – the rewards of all-out effort. It's time in your life, no matter your age, to do that again, only this time for your baby. My "dad friends" challenged me to do this, and they were right. Because of them, and their experi-ences, I lived this part of my life without regrets and fully engaged. Fortunately, I learned this lesson "on time," rather than "too late."

Resolve to be a "hands on" daddy. Start the minute the baby gets home from the hospital. Hold her, feed her (to the extent pos-sible), walk her, talk to her and change as many diapers as possible. I know, for some men this may be difficult.When my first child arrived home, I stared at him on the changing table in a state of perplexed helplessness. Where are the directions? Where's the step-by-step guidebook? For the first few days of life, highly trained, highly expe-rienced nurses cared for him. Now, he was looking up at me with those baby eyes going "waaah" and I was supposed to do what? This may sound silly, but in times of stress, I've repeated words or phrases in my mind that seemed to help get me through.This time was no exception (desperate times require desperate measures!). My words at this moment of truth:"Ha, baby, you don't scare me!" I repeated them many times!

To the moms, help and encourage the father to be involved. Bring him alongside, and show him how certain things are done. Show him how to hold a baby properly. Show him how to change a diaper. Make the baby experience a joy to be shared. If he seems a little reluctant, be patient and give him as much to do as he can handle. Catch him doing something right and complement him for being such a great dad. Use positive, empowering words. If you do this, you will be rewarded with a great "hands on" daddy. The love given to your baby will be without end and without limit.

Mom will be recovering from the birth, and sleep will be in short supply. It will be weeks before baby sleeps through the night. It helped me to remember that millions of humans before me had overcome the exhaustion and survived the experience. You're not the first and won't be the last. It's part of a life well lived. I thought of it like this: it was like being in college and staying up all night partying. Except there was no party and you couldn't sleep in the next day! Ouch! However, it's a time in your life for a special focus and special effort. Be there for each other as much as you can. Support each other. Laugh when there are any brief moments of humor. When conflict arises, realize you're both exhausted like never before and "it's not about me." And Dad – during this period, "mother knows best" is something to remember. Mom knows what baby needs, when baby needs it. So, support her during this baby time, unconditionally.

Beyond being fully engaged and fully committed to this top priority in your life, mom and dad must develop their own unique style of parenting. You're a family now, and you have the free will and spirit to decide how you are going to raise this gift from God. Remember the good things your parents did and throw out the bad and come up with a new plan. A better plan – yours. In order to develop a great plan, you need to read and learn. So, buy a lot of baby books and read together. Attend parenting classes, together. Seek out great parents (they're all around you) and ask how they did it. Find out what worked and what didn't work for them. Take all that great knowledge and, together with your own experiences, mold it into your own unique and great plan for parenting. Remember, as difficult as it may seem, you are not alone and help is only one friend or one phone call away. Finally, love your baby with all your heart and your entire mind.

How important is this? It's your one chance in life to write human history, one day at a time. Literally you are etching your child's memories with your words and actions. So, how good will it be? What will your children remember about you, their parents?

Don't underestimate the impact of simple things that you do with your children. My seven-year-old daughter has a vivid memory of our visit with friends in Montana last summer. I took my kids to Yellowstone and we saw wild buffalo, the canyons and the magic of an Old Faithful eruption. Out of all those amazing sights, she remembers the time she and I plopped down on the grass and watched the clouds go by. I asked her if she could identify the clouds by shape. Sure enough, there was a "doughnut," a "castle" and a "flower." It is stunning to me that, out of all the events in her life during the past year, she remembers the time we named the clouds.

LESSONS LEARNED LATE:

- Children are God's gift.

- A child will create a new dimension of love you never knew possible.

- You've never loved, and never been capable of loving, anything more than a baby.

- A baby depends on her parents for everything (one of the most sobering thoughts possible).

- For Dad, commit that, for the first year, the baby and her mother will be your top priority.

- Resolve to be a "hands on" daddy (Hey, baby, you don't scare me!).

- Mom and Dad must work together to develop their own unique style of parenting.

- Having a baby is your one chance to write human history.

- What will your children remember about you, their parents?

- Love your baby with all your heart and your entire mind.

- If you are successful at loving and laughing, the rest of parenting is not that serious!

27. BABY TURNS TWO/THREE

It's possible that your baby either was or will be perfect. She will sit in her crib and entertain herself. She will walk through the house, pick a few toys out of the toy box and play with them in the manner intended. She will listen to her parents and not severely test the limits of acceptable conduct. She will sit for meals and eat most of her vegetables in small bites. If this is your child, "hooray!" You are both lucky and blessed and there's no need to read any further. You can skip this part of the book.

My first son was none of these. I can remember holding my breath during his first few weeks in pre-school. Will he get kicked out? I was nervous when the teacher gave me his first report card: "He can't sit during circle time with the other children!" Yikes, I thought, a boy destined for a life of failure! Are there great colleges that don't require circle time, I wondered?

However, it didn't end there. Continuing my children's penchant for creativity, my second child collected toothbrushes and flashlights. He removed all the rubber tires from his many "miniature" toy trucks and stored them in a kitchen drawer. I couldn't make this up if I tried.

A. Water + Dirt

My first son would not sit in his crib and would not stand still. He was constantly on the go. He was fiercely independent and would say "me do it!" I'd try to carry him the way other parents would carry their kids, but he would squirm to get down and be set free. He's what the experts called, variously, "tactile" or "spirited." I thought he was "perpetually on the go" or "shot out of a cannon." I would call my older sister for advice, exasperated. She would tell me: "Freddy, you are smarter than a two year old!" I thought her confidence was misplaced and she didn't know me that well!

I asked his pre-school teacher who had years of experience what she advised. She said when all else fails, put them in the tub and run water out of the spout. Water is soothing, she explained, and it's the one activity that will capture their attention and keep them entertained on multiple sensory levels. I tried this and it seemed to work, but a bath only lasts a few minutes. What do you do with them the other twelve hours of the day? The only TV show he'd watch was Wheel of Fortune and his favorite letter was "T" which he'd yell out. I begged him to watch Sesame Street to no avail. No, there was no time for sittin. He liked to live life to the fullest "on the run."

Again, I'm no expert. All I can do is explain what I did when faced with this situation. This boy needed something that was in constant supply. Water outside and a place to dig. I gave him the end of a hose and turned the water on to a trickle. He would entertain himself for hours. He would pull the hose and water something, and then he'd pull it back and neatly curl it up. Then, he'd repeat it. Our trees and plants were tall and green that year!

I cleared a dirt area near the house, in the shade. I dug up the topsoil so he could easily work with the dirt. I told him this area was his "construction site" and his eyes got big. I showed him how to dig with a shovel and how to put the dirt in the bucket. Through the years, he's created elaborate "construction sites" with roads, bridges, tunnels and water features. Mostly, though, he just likes to dig. He's forever digging a hole and then filling it up with water. For him, digging plus water has been soothing to his soul and it's given him a creative outlet he desperately needed.

His skill with a shovel has come in handy lately. This spring, I said that since he liked to dig so much, he should clear an area and plant a garden. His eyes got big with excitement and he started immediately. I told him he could plant whatever he wanted. What did my thirteen-year old select? Pumpkins. That's right, we just harvested four pumpkins in time for the Fourth of July! We laughed that we could either advertise "Pumpkins For Sale," or we could have a pumpkin-carving contest. Where do you find pumpkin carving kits in July?

LESSONS LEARNED LATE:

- After you love them unconditionally, what do you actually do with the little ones to keep them entertained?

- Find activities that stimulate their senses.

- My sister always had a "bowling game" with paper cups stacked high and a ball to roll into them. Crash!

- Water is soothing and mud is magic.

- Create your own "construction site" and bring in the dump trucks and shovels.

- Put them in charge of the garden (and watch the pumpkins grow!).

B. Redirection and Discipline: It's as Easy as One, Two, Three!

He was digging. He was holding the hose with water dripping out. But it was time to go. How do you get little ones to stop what they are doing and redirect to another activity. How do you get them to listen to their parents? When I would ask politely, he'd ignore me. Once in a while, he'd stop what he was doing, but get distracted by another activity on the way to see me. Summoning all of my legal training, I had to come up with a plan to gradually get him to stop what he was doing (redirected) and follow my directions. I also needed to come up with a system of discipline that was effective for him. Not surprisingly, the regular methods of discipline had no effect. He'd either laugh or ignore me. I could see his little mind work and imagine what he was thinking behind that sly smile (Yes, Daddy, I'm a handful, and no, there's nothing you can do about it!).

Here's the system that worked for me. It's called "one, two, three, timeout." First, I give them the "two minute warning." Although small children don't have the ability to discern large increments of time, they can figure out that "two minutes" is a brief period of time. This puts them on alert that they should "wrap up" what they are doing. Is "two minutes" a magic number? No, I made it up and since I used it consistently, they understood what it meant. Then, starting with the child's name, I make a request that's clear and simple. I always say please. It might go like this: "Sparky, would you please stop digging and come inside and wash your hands for dinner." If Sparky does it right away I might say "What a great decision you made" or "Thank you for coming in so quickly" or just "Thank you." Since this seldom happened in the beginning, I would pause and then say "one." This tells the child the request is serious. If ignored, I say "two" and sometimes will even go to "two and one-half" if they are trying to comply. Once I get to "three," a "three" means Sparky gets a timeout. When they were very small, the timeout occurred in the nearest corner. They would stand there for maybe a minute (an eternity for a child) and then I'd ask them to say they were sorry and then go forward with the request (wash your hands for dinner). I would say "Thank you" and all would be forgotten.

This worked well for a while, but there were occasions when a timeout wasn't appropriate or the "punishment didn't fit the crime." For example, if the two boys couldn't agree on how to share a toy, my rule was the toy was gone. So, it gave them the power and responsibility to resolve the dispute on their own. If they couldn't, then the toy (or whatever object they were fighting over) was taken away. At first, this worked like a charm, but then I discovered that "out of sight was out of mind." If I grabbed the object and put it away, they'd forget about it and then argue about the next toy or object. I needed to do something that would remind them of the offending behavior and why it was better to get along.

From this necessity I created the "take away box." I found a small, sturdy brown box and told the boys that from now on, when they fought over a toy or used a toy in an inappropriate manner (throwing comes to mind), the toy or object would be immediately taken away and put in the "take away box." So, I would say "one, two, three," but, instead of them going for a time out, the consequence was the object was taken away and put in the box. It was placed on the floor in the kitchen for all to see. Since the box had a lot of use, I suggested that it should be colored and decorated, so it looked good. The boys liked that idea and scribbled on the sides. Over time, the decorating became more elaborate.

The "take away box" concept evolved over time. In my house, creativity tends to run wild, even on the subject of discipline. There were two more developments of note. Sometimes, the take away box was over flowing. Other times, there were some important items in the box (like their favorite dump truck without which, life was just too harsh)! So, I came up with another "rule." On some stuff, you could "earn it" back by doing a good deed or chore. Some-times it was cleaning something, other times it was doing a task they would enjoy, like running outside and watering the plants (anything, to run the water!). The boys really liked the concept of "earning" their stuff back. Obviously, it turned into an elaborate game (As you'll see later, a trend that continues to this day).

Finally, when their behavior was really awful, the boys were "on notice" that other more precious possessions would be taken away. The ultimate: their "blankys" were taken away and put in the box. It was sad, but the "punishment had to fit the crime," and sometimes they needed to understand the severity of their behavior. In case some reading this may think it too harsh, I never took their blan-kets away over night (Miraculously, they'd get them back in time to go to bed – often, by earning them back at the last minute before bedtime!).

To this day, the boys (now 13 and 11) will laugh about the take away box. They have vivid recollections of it and especially about putting their blankys in the box. "Remember the time our behavior was so bad we had to put our blankys in there" and then they'll howl with laughter.

LESSONS LEARNED LATE:

- It's about the behavior, not the child.
- Rules must be clear, age appropriate and consistently applied.
- A child needs help transitioning from one activity to another.
- Are your requests simple and clear?
- Always give them a choice between what you want them to do and something worse. Invariably, they'll decide that what you're asking isn't so bad and they'll comply.
- "One, two, three" gives the child an opportunity to decide to comply. If not, a "timeout" follows.
- Create a "take away box" for the object they were playing with when the offense occurred.
- Give the child a chance to earn their stuff back.
- Laugh and look them in the eye and say, "I love you."
- Redirect. "Hey, anybody want to drive to the ice cream store with the windows down?"

28. DECISIONS, DECISIONS

During the first two to three years, parents will be faced with a number of decisions about child rearing. The challenges range from TV time and content to maintaining a schedule to whether the child can sleep in the parents' bed. The exciting part is that as parents, you get to make the rules and decide how the child will be raised. Each family is unique and yours is no exception. This is a moment of freedom of choice. You can look back on your own life and figure out what you liked, and didn't like, about your own childhood. You should read parenting books, together as a couple, and discuss what you like and what's important. Be prepared to be flexible, because parenting is all about listening, learning and compromise. It's also important to attend parenting classes and ask friends you respect for their opinion. How are they doing it? While it may be daunting at first, parents will soon get comfortable mapping out the child issues that are important and those that matter less.

I'll discuss a few that I faced, ranging from the silly to serious. The first surprise was that none of my children wanted a pacifier. I thought it must be a great invention and every infant must have one. Feeling obligated, I gave the pacifier to each and their response was the same. "Pa-tooey," out it came. I would "plug" and they would spit, until I gave up. This proved to be a blessing in disguise because I couldn't figure out what it was supposed to do (although I did notice improvements in design over the years). It was one less thing to remember and one less item to lose. It was also one less habit they had to "break" as they grew older.

The next challenges were about schedule, bedtime and whether they could sleep in their parents' bed. The parenting books encourage parents to establish a routine and a schedule. Bedtime is always the same time (eight p.m.) and the routine is the same, with a bedtime story to end the evening. Miraculously, this proved to be great advice and I didn't experience any of the bedtime traumas that other parents have described. I also followed the advice of "sleep in your own bed" and not with your parents. While difficult on the parents at the moment of crisis, I believe this promoted their development towards self-confidence and self esteem.

Another probably less discussed issue is fear. As the child grows older, he/she will begin to interact with strangers. There's no question it's a jungle out there and a child must learn to be cautious. A child must be taught and guided on issues of safety and the fact that "you should not accept candy from a stranger." As they get older the phrase evolves into "stranger danger." However, I want my kids to be secure and self-confident. I've raised them to be self reliant and good decision makers. I did not want them to be fearful of the world outside or fearful of others. Cautious and safe, yes, but fearful, no. I never discussed fear with them and instead, wanted them to be happy children enjoying their childhood. I'll admit I erred on the side of encouraging them to be fearless and approach life with a smile. If you asked them to discuss the subject of fear, I believe they'd look at you with a blank stare. They wouldn't understand. And I'd be pleased. If I've been deficient as a parent because I didn't discuss or explain the subject of fear enough with them, I'm prepared to admit it and accept the consequences.

To be sure, you'll have "ups and downs" and struggles, but stick with the routine and eventually the child will find comfort. Finally, it's important not to take the little things too seriously. If you love them and hug them, the child will survive and prosper despite your foibles. For example, I was curious what my first-born would dream about and if he slept well. One morning he said he dreamt about "butterflies and bees" and I thought he either actually dreamt about them or associated them with "sweet dreams." Thereafter, I would ask if he dreamed about "butterflies and bees" and he would say "yes." Recently, I asked him what he remembered and do you know what he said? "Butterflies and bees" were just words that meant nothing. He made them up and repeated them only because he thought I liked to hear the words! Smart child, silly father!

LESSONS LEARNED LATE:

- Parenting is a chance to "re-do" your childhood.

- Remember the best and throw out the "not so good."

- Celebrate your unique new family and blaze a new trail.

- Read books, attend parenting classes, and ask your friends and family for advice.

- Listen, learn and compromise. Parenting is a journey, not a destination.

- Both parents must agree in advance on the parenting "game plan." This takes time, so get started.

- Love them and hug them (and love and hug each other in front of them!).

- It's not that serious. Laugh often.

29. CREATIVE DISCIPLINE

A. The Middle is No Place To Be

As any parent knows, raising kids is tough. I joke that it's a full contact sport. Any time there's two or more kids involved in an activity, there's bound to be disputes. And that is putting it mildly. Parenting young children seems more like being a manager of professional wrestling.

I had a difficult time managing the three kids when they were young. The types of problems and disputes they had seemed to be in endless supply. Can't they just play quietly, I'd wonder to no one in particular? My tendency was to get in the middle and try to help them work it out. Then I'd get really frustrated and the situation would seem to go from bad to worse. At these dark times of fatherhood, I'd call my sister for advice. "Sharon, they are running wild and bickering constantly! What should I do?" There'd be a moment of silence as she thought the situation through and then she'd yell at me. "Freddy, stay out of it! The middle is no place to be!" On a roll, she'd continue "You cannot solve their problems for them. If you try, you'll become a part of the childishness and it'll never end. Stay out of it!" Ouch. It's not easy to be yelled at by your sister, but she was right. Whenever I got involved there'd be more arguing, blaming and "he did this/he did that." They had to solve their problems themselves.

If you watch pre-school teachers, they are adept at handling this challenge. If one child has a problem, they will ask her to "use words" to explain the situation. They will ask her to explain what happened and how she feels as a result. They will then direct the child to explain this to the offender. In no time, each child learns to use words to express their feelings and "claim them" as legitimate. They also learn to say, "I'm sorry" for what they did. Then, in a flash, their smiles return and they skip off together eager to resume their play. All's forgotten, quickly.

As an aside, pre-school teachers use highly descriptive words. "Inside voice." "Use your walking feet." "Is that a toy?" They will mix it up by sometimes asking questions. "Who has their listening ears on?" I've always wanted to try this last request on a group of lawyers and watch their utterly perplexed reaction. Lawyers with listening ears? Seems improbable, doesn't it?

My problem, of course, is that I'm not as good as my sister and I'm certainly not as good as a pre-school teacher. I'm an imperfect Daddy trying my best to manage myself first (hey, I'll admit it!). Desperate, and with limited skills, I've taken the simple approach. When my three have a dispute I tell them to "use words and work it out." If they continue bickering (and he said/she said), I'll repeat, "use words and work it out." As a last resort, I'll tell them "If you can't use words and work it out, the activity is gone." Amazingly, when they realize I'm not getting involved and they face the prospect of losing their activity, they resolve the problem and return to play. An upside is that, over the years, they've become very close and I know each believes they couldn't live without the others.

LESSONS LEARNED LATE:

- The middle is no place to be.
- Stay out of children disputes (do you want to be a referee for life?).
- Tell the children to "use words" and work it out.
- They should learn to express their feelings and "claim them" as legitimate.
- They should also learn to say, "I'm sorry."
- If you can't use words and work it out, the activity is gone.
- Praise them with positive words after they've worked it out.

B. Good Heaven, He's Seven: Money Matters

My system of discipline was working until about age 7. At this age, my kids were maturing to the "next level" and needed more independence and responsibility. This meant I had to figure out what mattered to them and what would motivate them. They were also asking for more things at the store and these items were getting more expensive. If he would ask for something and I just said "no," there wasn't any logic to it and no boundaries were created. The more desperate he was for the item/toy, the more he'd try to whine to get it. Also, he had no appreciation for how much things cost and how fortunate he was to get something. The words "budget" or "spending limit" didn't seem to register in his little mind. Finally, I wanted him to do extra chores around the house and take on more household responsibilities.

I decided that the way to motivate him and instill responsibility was to give him an allowance. The first challenge was to figure out the amount. I have three kids and, as little lawyers, they are acutely aware of "fairness." If one got something, they all wanted the same thing. There were many times when I brought "three" of something home so they all received the same item and wouldn't argue or feel bad. I'm sure every parent with two or more children has been in the same position. To avoid this problem, I decided to give them an allowance equal to their age. Since they understood they were different ages, an allowance equal to their age made sense. Logic trumped any feeling of unfairness. "Payday" was set for Sunday and they get a "raise" on the Sunday after their birthday.

There are many books advocating an allowance and I encourage you to read them. The experts will go into great detail about the benefits of an allowance. Some of the experts even propose a more elaborate system in which the kids get an allowance, but then must divide it into "threes." One part savings, one part "taxes" to help pay the costs of the household and one part that must be given to charity. This will teach the child important lessons about money management and the costs and responsibilities of being an adult. I tried this initially, but my son didn't grasp the nuances. Rather than try to stay with the system of "threes" that didn't hold his interest, I decided to let him save all of his money for himself. I may try again when he's older, but for now he puts his money in a jar and watches it accumulate (literally piling up in the clear jar).

I've talked with other parents who tried the allowance program, but ran into difficulties. Some stopped after a period of time when the child would not do her chores. They would take money away and deduct some amount from her allowance if certain chores weren't completed. In the child's mind, her allowance became associated with another means of punishment and amounts were randomly being deducted. Alternatively, "pay day" was skipped altogether, with the allowance being "offset" by other expenses. This could occur, for example, when the child wants something at a store and then negotiates an "offset" with the parent. The child would plead "Let me have this seven dollar toy on Wednesday and you don't need to pay me my allowance next Sunday." The parent would say "OK" and the deal was struck, but diminishing the importance of their money and the consequences of their decision-making in the process.

When dealing with any kid issue, a parent has to establish rules that are simple and clear and then enforce them with consistency. No doubt it's a challenge, but the "lessons learned" by the child in the home are invaluable, especially fundamental ones like decisions have consequences and there are limits and we all must live with them. In my case, the learning has evolved over time and has required some "quick thinking" at times. However, parents must be prepared to "say what you mean, and mean what you say." A child's job is to test limits and probe for weakness, so the parent must be firm and consistent. Yes, it's difficult to face off against a sobbing little one, but have you noticed how quickly their moods change and they move on to something else? I had the added benefit of hearing my sister's voice saying "Freddy, you are smarter than a two-year-old!"

The first benefit associated with their allowance was that it stopped the whining for a toy at the supermarket (or similar store). Before the allowance, the child would "I want" everything and there was no way to encourage them to stop or limit their requests. After, I could say "You have a choice: you have an allowance and this toy costs seven dollars, so if you want to spend all your money on this toy, go ahead, it's your decision." Suddenly, the toy didn't look so appealing and having it wasn't so urgent. It completely changed the power dynamics. It wasn't "me against them" anymore, it was "you have the power to make these decisions and you will suffer the consequences of your decision." I was surprised at how quickly they caught on when the power struggle was taken out of the equation.

As the weeks passed and their money piled up in their jar, I discovered something shocking (admittedly, I'm a slow learner). The only thing that mattered to my kids was their own money. They'd spend mine all day long and never appreciate it. I was feeding the insatiable "I want" machine whenever I spent my money. However, their attitude was totally different when what they were spending was theirs. I'd give them choices and they'd think long and hard about whether to give in to impulse and spend their money. I discovered their secret. Money did matter, but only if it was theirs!

LESSONS LEARNED LATE:

- Parents must establish rules that are simple and clear. Apply them with consistency.

- Say what you mean and mean what you say.

- Always give them choices.

- Change the power dynamics: suggest they use their own money

- Give them an allowance equal to their age (payday's on Sunday)

- If they want a toy, they can make the choice and spend their own money.

- There's only one thing that matters: their own money.

- Discover this secret of the children universe and the power is yours!

C. Additional Allowance Insights

I have some additional thoughts and experiences to share on the allowance subject. Like virtually everything else in this book, I've learned these lessons after trial and error. The most important principal is to set the rules and follow them. This means both parents must be "on board" and prepared to consistently apply the rules. Obviously, one parent will undermine the system if they readily give the child extra money, buy the child anything they want and/or never confront the child with the "spend your own money" choices. An allowance and the choices/consequences that follow are so effective because it operates like real life. A responsible, well-adjusted adult understands there are limits and priorities. Budgets must be established and then respected. Delayed or deferred gratification is an important attribute in a balanced life. With an allowance, a child is learning many valuable lessons on their own terms at an early age. They are fully capable of making great decisions, so supply the opportunity and be prepared to be amazed at how well they manage.

A child will benefit when his early life lessons reflect reality. To that end, an allowance provides a wealth (pun intended!) of learning opportunities. Recently, my boys have been saving up for some items they desperately want. The conversation with one of them went like this. "Daddy, I want a metal airplane." I said he had his own money and, if that's what he wanted to spend his hard-earned money on, that was up to him. I asked how much the plane cost and he said thirty-five dollars. I said that's a lot of money for a toy, but it's your decision. Then I asked how much money he had and he said twenty-five dollars (he had to buy birthday presents for his siblings and his money was depleted at the moment). He said he wanted to buy it that evening and asked me if I'd take him to the mall. I said no, because he didn't have enough money. He then pleaded and whined about how desperate he was to get the toy and how long he'd waited. He then asked if he could buy the toy and have me deduct the difference from his allowance next Sunday. I said no, you don't get an advance on your allowance and "payday" is on Sunday. He then asked if I'd loan him the money and he could repay me on Sunday. I'll admit I was impressed with his negotiating skills. I said, "Son, I'm not a bank and you don't have a credit card. You can't borrow allowance money from me and you can't decide to go into debt. It doesn't work that way for you now or when you're an adult. I can't go to my boss and ask for more money." If you want something, I explained, you must earn your allowance and save up the cash to buy what you want. He said, OK, he'd wait until Sunday and then use his allowance. I then said, "Is sales tax charged when you buy something?" He said, yes, and asked how much it was. I estimated eight percent and then we turned it into a math problem and together figured out the approximate amount of sales tax. I then said he needed to save an additional amount to pay the cost in full, including sales tax, and he needed to give the sales clerk the full amount in cash. To his credit, he listened and ultimately agreed. An hour later, he said something even more amazing. "Daddy, I've thought about it, and that plane isn't worth spending all my money on. I'm going to wait and buy a toy that doesn't cost so much, so I have some money left." Wow, a lesson I hoped he would learn, but one he had to teach himself. Faced with a decision, he carefully thought about it and decided, on his own, what was best. I doubt he would have learned this lesson so early or so clearly if he was spending my money. In fact, I'm convinced he would not have made the same decision if I were offering to pay. As important, he learned this lesson without the typical power struggle with his dad.

LESSONS LEARNED LATE:

- Children should make their own decisions with their allowance money.

- Both parents must be "on board" and not undermine the allowance system (it'll be challenging at times).

- No advances, no credit. Cash only.

- "I'm not a bank and you don't have a credit card."

- If they run out of money, it's their problem. They must suffer the consequences. Parents are out of the equation.

- They must count their money and take cash to pay the sales clerk.

- They must budget for other expenses, such as buying birthday presents for parents/siblings.

- Encourage them to be charitable and give their money to church or charity.

30. TEACHING MANNERS

I believe it's important for children to have manners. I'm from Nebraska and that's the way I was raised. It was even worse in my family, because Dad was in retailing and if his customers weren't treated well and respected, his business would evaporate. No customers, no money to pay the bills. It was as simple as that. Manners and respect became a non-negotiable priority.

How do you teach manners to your children? I started by asking them to say "please" and "thank you." It worked for a while, but it became tiring to remind them. Slightly enlightened, I thought it might be a good idea to model the behavior I wanted them to display. So, I started to say "please" and "thank you" whenever I asked them to do something or whenever they did something for me. This worked fairly well and I continue it to this day. But there were times when they'd forget and I didn't want to be in the habit of constantly reminding them to be polite. Intellectually, it seemed incongruous for me to impolitely remind them to be polite. The word "nagging" comes to mind. My challenge was to figure out how to encourage them to be polite (use the magic words!) without having to remind them.

Summoning all of my legal training, I concluded that I couldn't control what they said, but I could control how I reacted. Simply, the only power I had was the power to respond. If their request is not made with an appropriate tone of voice and does not include one of the "magic words," I have the ability not to respond or refuse to give them what they want. To this day, if they ask me something without being polite, I won't respond, won't do it or will say "no." If they say, "Can I have some milk" (or worse, whine or demand to get what they want), I'll say "no." They pause and smile and say "Can I please have some milk" and I smile and say "yes!" It works like a charm and has taken the power struggle out of the equation. I get what I want (polite children) and they eventually get what they were asking for (well, most of the time!). Of course, we've turned this into an elaborate game and it works especially well on my thirteen-year-old who's discovered he enjoys wearing his "smarty pants" at times.

LESSONS LEARNED LATE:

- Children should have good manners and be respectful.

- The "magic words" are please and thank you.

- Model the behavior you want to see and include "please" in your requests to them.

- If they are not being polite, make it clear you will ignore their request or say "no."

- Wait for them to re-phrase their request. A "please" will get you a "yes!" (Most of the time!)

- Turn manners into a game.

31. KIDS GROW UP AND NEW PROBLEMS ARISE

A. A New Life After Divorce

Unfortunately, when my three kids were about ages 6 to 12, I got a divorce. It was not something I wanted, but it became a reality and I had to deal with it. A divorce with children presents many challenges, some I was prepared for and many I was not. My character and spirit were seriously tested and I had to quickly figure out how to act. My children were intently focused on my words and deeds. A father is a powerful example in a child's life and I needed to "step up" to the challenge. They didn't vote for this situation and didn't want to hear about my problems. They had a ruptured childhood that needed to be mended, so they could return to living a happy, loving, secure childhood. The bottom line: When they reach adulthood, they must look back and say "Daddy, even though you and Mom got divorced and it wasn't easy, I always knew you loved me and I had happy times whenever I was with you. I still had a happy childhood." A tall order, to be sure. I constantly prayed for strength and wisdom, because both seemed in short supply.

I attended parenting classes to learn about life as a divorced parent with three young children. The message was direct and simple. "It's not about you," the psychologist told the class. She wrote it on the board. She asked us to write it into our memory. Whatever happened between you and your ex doesn't matter. The problems of the past are irrelevant. The children don't want to hear it. They have a busy job being children and trying to sort through the wreckage. They've lost their home and their parents living together as an intact family and now have a life filled with anger, grief, sadness, regret, blame and a whole lot more.

The good news is that children are highly resilient and can adjust to a new life of separate parents with separate homes. They have basic needs of wanting to be loved unconditionally and feeling emotionally secure. As a divorced parent, your entire focus and mindset must shift to "it's not about you." When you do, you'll be in a frame of mind to make your love abundant and their new life as normal as possible. It's all about "what's best for the children."

One of the decisions I had was, where do I live? I didn't need much in the short term, but I needed to find a place suitable for children. Where would they play? Equally important to my kids, where would they dig? I found the ideal solution. I rented a 1970's "tear down" house on a large lot. The back yard was huge and there were plenty of places for them to dig. I immediately introduced them to the house and pointed proudly to a spot of dirt, "here's your new construction site!" I then went to the hardware store and bought three new shovels. They were in business.

This house taught us many lessons. A house is just "stuff" and "stuff" doesn't matter. People matter. When life doesn't go your way, laugh at the situation and make fun of it. The added joy was that the house was indestructible. It's like being freed from the shackles of perfection. The other day, my oldest boy was bouncing a ball on the floor and he said, in a mocking voice, "Oh no, I'm bouncing a ball on the floor! On no, I bumped the wall! I might need some paint to repair the wall!" We laughed and laughed because this was not a "normal" house and there's nothing that could be harmed. The children know they are safe and secure here, and are allowed to live as kids without unnecessary worries. They know they are the most important priority in my life. Everything else, is just stuff. Permanent markers for the walls, anyone?

LESSONS LEARNED LATE:

- Don't let a divorce ruin a childhood.
- No matter the cause, "it's not about you."
- It is about what's best for the children.

- A divorced parent's goal: As young adults, they can look back on their childhood and say, "Even though you got divorced, I still had a happy childhood. I knew you loved me and I was happy each time I was with you."

- Children/people matter. Everything else is just stuff.

- Free yourself from the shackles of perfection.

- Important words: "Can you play, Daddy?"

B. Crowd Control

I believed it was important to keep things the same. I tried to cook the same meals and feed them the same healthy food. I had the same rules for discipline and the same rules about their allowance and money. I told them I loved them, frequently. I told them I was proud of them when they made good decisions. I set the bar high and gave them extra responsibilities in my house. I expected them to continue to treat their siblings and others with respect. I didn't talk about others and have never said a negative word about their mother. While I felt guilty during the early period of divorce, I didn't act upon my feelings. I didn't buy them any extra toys or try to "make up" for the way life was unfolding. It "was what it was" and we were going to make the best of it. My love for them each was unconditional and I demonstrated that with my words and hugs and kisses.

Our new life together was working fairly well until I ran into a big problem. Based on a combination of the affects of the divorce, their new living situation with their mother, three children vying for attention, and getting older, they would arrive at my house bickering and saying words I didn't approve of. It was very frustrating and I didn't know what to do about it. I tried to explain that their words weren't appropriate, but they would ignore me. My oldest was becoming a teenager and his hormones were raging. The others were perfecting the art of arguing, whining and yelling for what they wanted or needed. In many ways, I suppose it's the typical path of progression for three children growing up together, but it was made worse by the situation. I wasn't around all the time to encourage consistent behavior and their words reflected it. I was at a loss.

After trying everything else, I told them in clear and simple words that their behavior was unacceptable. They were acting in a way that was inappropriate. I asked them, "Is this the way you talk to your teachers at school? Is this the way you behave in your classroom?" Their answer, of course, was no. It seems children always save their worst behavior for those they love the most. Their family! I then told them their words were a choice. They were old enough to understand they were making a choice and it wasn't a good one. However, the choice is theirs and I can't change it. While I had no power over their words and behavior, I did not have to either like it or approve of it. And I told them so. But that, of course, would have no lasting impact on their daily choices of "bad words/bad behavior." I had to find something that mattered to them. It took me a long time to figure out what that was. Again, my legal training turned in handy.

I reaffirmed that words spoken were choices and they needed to make better ones in my house. I know they heard "blah, blah, blah" and were undaunted. Then, I threw the curve ball. "From now on, you will pay to play. I can't prevent you from saying bad words, but I can sure charge you for them! I will charge you twenty-five cents for every bad word and you will pay me out of your allowance money you've saved. I will put the quarter into a "bad word" jar. There will also be a "whining" jar and you will each be charged twenty-five cents for whining."

They were stunned. Money was important to them and was the only thing that mattered. Then, my quick-thinking middle child said, "Daddy, what are you going to do with all that money you collect?" I thought a moment, impressed by his ability to grasp the big picture and do the math (translated: our collective words are so awful, you're going to be rich!). I replied "we're going to save up the money and give it to the poor children at church." And so was borne an elaborate game called the "whining jar," complete with a twist I would've never imagined.

As I've mentioned before, I'm raising little lawyers. I have no idea what career they'll eventually pursue, but it's clear they are honing their lawyer skills at a very young age. Having captured both their attention and their imagination with the whining jar, all four of us were engaged and ready for debate. We needed rules in place so everyone knew what to expect. They each had a clear understanding of what "whining" was, so I established a separate whining jar. I give them a warning, and then, with them being on clear notice of a pending violation, I impose the twenty-five cent cost for the next bout of whining. They must pay immediately (no credit cards allowed) and they must place their own money in the jar. Being a great Daddy, I'm always available to make change! Our first jar was in place and coins were filling the bottom of the jar.

The "bad word" jar took more time and was far more elaborate to develop. The boys would walk into my house saying the word "crap." I didn't like that word spoken in my house, so I told them, in the future, that word would cost them twenty-five cents. Old habits die hard and one time my middle child said the word, then said the word again in frustration, then said the word a third time in indignation. He holds the record for the most consecutive fines in the least amount of time. Seventy-five cents was lost in less than a minute. For other words, we've had to discuss and all agree that the word is, indeed, bad. Borrowing from criminal procedure and the constitutional guarantee of "procedural due process," a word is not "bad" until after the time of agreement. All of us must discuss, negotiate and agree that the offending word is added as a "bad" word. Only then does the utterance cost a quarter. We've had many lively discussions on this topic and sometimes we can't get complete agreement. We continue to compromise until all agree. Other words added include name calling (stupid, idiot), inappropriate ones (suck) and mean ones (I hate you).

The third jar is the "yelling" jar. I don't like them to yell at each other and I wanted them to stop. So I told them that, after a warning, yelling would cost a quarter. Then the most amazing twist occurred that I was totally unprepared for. The kids said that these were "house" rules that should apply to everyone. Even me! I said they were right and I agreed. All the rules and all the principles apply to me. Even if there's a word I say that they don't like, they can bring it up for discussion and, if we all agree, the offending word is added. Sometimes I yell when their behavior goes over the line. I know I shouldn't do it, but sometimes the words escalate. In this case, the rules apply to me and I must deposit twenty-five cents in the jar.

Now, when the boys are going at it and I yell to get them to stop, the first thing my oldest boy says while looking me straight in the eye is "That'll cost you twenty-five cents for yelling!" I huff and I puff and I say, "You're right," and then walk away and deposit a quarter in the jar. It immediately calms everyone down and breaks the power struggle. They react with a certain glee. Having all the rules apply to me has been profound. The kids believe the power has equalized and a sense of "fairness" or justice prevails. The difference in their behavior has been remarkable. I would've never imagined the positive impact this has had on my family. Now, we are equal and my power over them has been taken away and transferred to them. They now have more respect for the game, for each other, and surprisingly, for me. Our relationship has taken a wonderful turn for the better, while correcting some behavior that needed to be changed. I'm happy, they're happy. Oh, and in the latest development, I told my pastor about my game and he said, "That's not fair, you should be charged a dollar!" I conveyed the story to the kids and they agreed. Yes, the yelling jar has a few of Daddy's greenbacks in it!

LESSONS LEARNED LATE:

- Words are a choice.

- Choices have consequences.

- I can't prevent you from making poor choices, but I can make you pay for them.

- The Whining Jar: Whining will cost ya twenty-five cents.

- The "Bad Word" Jar: Once we agreed on the offending words, each will cost twenty-five cents.

- The Yelling Jar: If you yell, you must stop and pay immediately (a great way to cool off).

- All rules apply to me (with the amount recently increased to one dollar for Daddy).

- I've been stunned by the impact of the shift in the balance of power.

- With rules applying equally, the children have a sense of justice. It's not "power over" it's "power equal."

- They enforce the rules against me, and I immediately comply.

- Parent/child relationship has taken a dramatic turn for the better.

- Start your own jar and watch the fun begin (and behavior change!).

32. THESE REQUIRE LITTLE EXPLANATION

A. Help Your Children Find Their Passion

It's not about you. Your job as parent is to help your child discover his/her passion. As individuals, we're all different. The activities you enjoy may not get your child excited. Your objective is to find sports they might like or activities that match their personality. Expose them to different musical instruments and different subjects at school. This may take time and require a sampling of many activities. My oldest likes tennis and the trumpet and wants to be an engineer so he can work with his hands. He recently discovered he enjoys distance running. My middle son likes baseball, tennis and the trombone. My youngest likes "swimming fast" and making crafts. It's unlikely any of them will be a high school star, but they enjoy what they're doing and seem proud when they do well or advance to the next level. So far, they seem well adjusted because, in part, they are already making their own way in life. My wish for them is that, like my Dad, they will "love what they do so they'll never work a day in their lives."

B. Prepare Them to Try and Fail

The ability to try and fail is an important life skill. While failure is often painful, it is the ultimate teacher. How much have you learned from your successes? How memorable are the times in your life when everything went perfect and you succeeded? If you're like me, I suspect your answers would be "not much" and "not very." No, the truth is, I needed the hard lessons to knock me down, then I had to learn how to pick myself up, dust myself off, and get back in the contest. These lessons were necessary to give me the foundation for who I am today.

It's no different with your children. The sooner they can learn how to try and how to fail, the better off they'll be. I want my kids to learn failure gently, in age appropriate doses. To do that, I want them to start at an early age. There's nothing more difficult for a parent than to stand back and watch as your child struggles and then fails. But watch you must, for the child must develop a healthy attitude about failure and the hard work it takes to overcome obstacles in life. When they're older, my goal is for them to call me after they've tried and failed (not before) and to talk about how they made the decision and what they think they could do better next time. My hope is they'll have many lessons learned on time.

C. Catch Them Doing Something Right

Pre-school teachers are terrific at encouraging positive behavior and catching children "doing something right." While they apply gentle correction, their attention is not turned away until the child has completed the task the right way and then been rewarded for their success. If you listen carefully, you will hear the teacher ask, while at eye level, "What could you have done better" or say, "That was a great job of trying, and you finally made it!" Patient, positive reinforcement abounds.

As parents, at least for me, it seems we are the hardest on our own children. Other parents/teachers comment about how polite they are, etc., but we're only focused on what's wrong. Nine things could go right, but it's the one "wrong" thing that we bring to our own child's attention. I've been working hard lately to change this and "catch them doing something right." I can see the change in their facial expressions when I use positive words. I even tell them "You've been doing a great job of making decisions lately" and "Doesn't that feel good to you?" I could go on, but you get the picture. I want to be positively encouraged and I know they feel the same way.

D. Look For Teachable Moments

Did you listen to your parents when you were young? Do your kids stand straight and listen intently when you are talking to them? In both cases, the answer is no. Kids have many jobs, and one of them seems to be running away from the words and influence of their parents. They are struggling to establish their independence and individuality, and the battle starts with the ones they love the most, their parents. It was that way for you, it's that way for them and so it will continue. Mark Twain seemed to capture the essence when he said: "When I was seventeen, I couldn't believe what a fool my father was, and by twenty-seven, I couldn't believe how much he'd learned in only ten years!"

Does that mean you don't try? No, it means that, as a thinking adult, you need to develop creative ways to communicate and teach your children the life lessons they need to learn "on time." Effective teachers look for (or create) teachable moments. They allow the student to share the sense of exploration, but then use the situation to explain important concepts like "poor choices will produce poor consequences."

For example, my town makes liberal use of photo radar. The trucks are hidden on the side of the road behind the bushes, and when you're zipping along at 6 miles over the speed limit, "bang" the radar is tripped and the lights flash like you're a movie star on the red carpet. You have the abrupt sense of fame, except for all the wrong reasons. Yup, your speeding ticket will soon be speeding its way to your mailbox. Since we see this on most days I drive them to school, we've had many conversations about photo radar and the consequences of speeding. After seeing a yellow Corvette zip by and get flashed, I explained that, not only must you pay the fine and court costs (they make you pay to go to court?), but your car insurance rates go up too. Thus, speeding is not only unsafe, but it's very expensive. So, if you're sixteen years old and on a tight budget, how will you earn more money to pay the higher cost of insurance? I also explained that you can't drive without car insurance and if the price goes up, you're not getting anything more for your money. Since they get an allowance (and must pay for whining and bad words!), they really understand that spending more of your allowance money for nothing in return is not a good deal.

Look for teachable moments and share stories with your kids. Allow them to walk down the path of exploration with you and then talk about the lessons you learned late, but you hope they learn on time. Explain that life provides a multitude of opportunities with choices and a good life is built on good choices. Also explain that the choices they make are theirs and the consequences will follow. Always end on a positive note, expressing the positive thought that you know they've been making great decisions and you know that will continue.

Finally, try to explain that life isn't perfect and neither are we. Expect difficult things to happen and be prepared to "bounce back." You can't control what happens, but you can control how you react. I recently got the opportunity to share my own teachable moment. "Hey kids, Daddy's house was just torn down! Want to go see a giant track-hoe sitting on top of the rubble?" Excited, we hopped in the car and sped towards the site of my former house. I grabbed my camera and assembled the three kids for a pose in front of the debris. My seven-year-old daughter yelled out "Hey Daddy, this can be our Christmas photo!" Great idea, but what words of holiday cheer should be added next to the picture?

E. If You Want Them to Value Something, You Must Value It First

Children are attuned to their parents. They are incredibly perceptive. They can easily sense your moods and feel the vibrations of your soul. They take meaning from your facial expressions and tone of voice. Since a parent figure is so powerful, it comes as no surprise that a child learns about life first from their parents. The early lessons are learned by example. Then, additional lessons are added by words conveyed. The learning never stops for a child and continues into adulthood. They watch and learn every minute of every day. It's sobering, indeed, to comprehend the level of responsibility a parent has for a child.

While there are adult activities and child activities, I believe a child has a difficult time understanding those nuances. I think a child just watches, looks and listens to the world around them and begins to form opinions about how to act, what to do, and what is important. For example, if the big lessons are to be kind and respectful and not to "lie, cheat and steal," then the child is watching what the parents do in each of these categories. Is that how you live your life? Are you the example you want your children to follow and emulate? Do you value the things you're telling them to value? If you want them to be punctual, are you always on time or are you perpetually a few minutes behind? If you want them to be calm, do you rush them from activity to activity and impatiently yell at the other drivers who get in your way? Both literally and figuratively, are you telling them not to smoke as you light up and puff away?

I know this is easy to talk about, but difficult to implement. It's a struggle. I'm certainly not perfect and I fall short. However, since my kids are getting more mature, I've been asking myself lately whether I'm truly valuing what I want them to value. Am I living up to my end of the bargain? I'm not sure, but I'm trying hard to be the example I want them to follow. Why? Because I know they're watching me far more intently than I'm watching them. I know my actions speak and my actions teach, whether I'm fully aware at the moment or not.

F. The Car Radio is Off

Like most kids, my children are active and always on the go. When they were young, I tried to engage them in conversation but it was difficult. We could make it through a few words, but I had a hard time getting them to share their thoughts or feelings. I was frustrated because I wanted to know what they were thinking and how they perceived the world around them. I also found that I couldn't predict when they'd be in the mood to talk. Often, they'd be tired or simply have nothing to say. Then, as I was toting them from place to place, I discovered the magic of a car ride. They were strapped in their car seat and going nowhere. I had their focus and attention. I could ask them questions and they would answer, sometimes with words and sometimes with complete sentences.

So, I decided to turn the radio off. That's right, I've never played the radio while there's a kid in the car (and rarely talk on the cell phone). There's nothing to distract us from talking. And we've had the most amazing conversations. Sometimes it's about my favorite car topic, construction equipment. We talk about the different types and the job each one is best at. I point out how the equipment forms a team, with each one relying on the other. We also talk about "cool cars" and have even developed an elaborate "car game." Looking back, the best and deepest conversations I've had with my kids have occurred in the car.

On some occasions, there's just silence. I'll ask them during the quiet times if they're tired and they'd say "yes." So, we drive merrily down the road in complete silence. With our lives so active and with constant noise, I figure a little silence, a little down time, can be a very good thing. Recently, my middle child asked if I even liked music, because the radio's never on. I said "Oh, I love music, but I love talking to you in the car even more!"

Turn your car radio off and talk to your kids. There's no distraction and nothing else to do. You'll be amazed and rewarded with their deepest thoughts. The only other possibility is silence and even that's not so bad!

G. No, You Can't Quit Spanish (Pick Your Battles)

As my children grow older, I'm trying to give them more responsibilities and more decisions. As they gain their independence, they're better able to express themselves. When they were small, you told them something and they did it. Now when I tell them to do something, they object and explain why they'd either not like to do it or suggest an alternative. Some plain-talking folks might call this "argu-ing" and "some" might be right! However, the kids are growing up and if they are expressing their beliefs, feelings etc., they deserve to be heard. They deserve to be listened to and respected. It's not easy and it's not perfect, but I can tell they're relieved when I've paused to listen and consider their views. I've even found that, some-times, they are "right" and their instant response is actually quite thoughtful.

I've decided it's important to "pick my battles." There are some big issues/decisions that I know are good for them and I'm not going to budge. For example, after taking Spanish for years, my son recently said he "wanted to quit." I understand why he wants to quit, because it's a difficult subject for him. I explained that quitting was not an option, because he's come so far and he should learn to speak two languages. I've even used the dreadful parent words that "Some day you'll thank me for this!" However, on issues of lesser importance, I've tried to listen and allow the children to influ-ence me. I've decided that, unless it's a "big/nonnegotiable" issue, I'm going to listen to their arguments. Sometimes I even let the little lawyers talk me out of something they should be doing if I know they genuinely don't want to do it. Making them do something when they're tired, for example, is not going to help them. On small mat-ters, it's more important that they know their feelings have been expressed and they've periodically "won the day." I'll be the first to admit it's not been easy and challenges abound. I should post a sign: "Hey Little Lawyers: Whining won't work, but thoughtful words will be considered!"

H. Yes, You're Being Raised to Move Out

There are many articles written about "boomerang kids." These are the young men and women who graduate from college, get a job and move back in with mom and dad. Sometimes they finally move out on their own by age 30 and sometimes they don't. My kids haven't read the articles nor are they aware of the trend (yet). I'm raising my kids to be independent, interesting and interested adults.

With their independence of spirit comes independence of household as well. I want my kids looking forward to an exciting future.

One of the great experiences of youth is moving out on your own. You did it. I did it. They should do it. It's good for them. Nothing will make you grow up faster and make better decisions than when you start living on your own. I've seen the benefits of responsibility already. My kids act and react much different when it's their own money and their own effort is involved. So, kids, get out there and enjoy life on your own. Yes, I'll stop by and visit (and bring some healthy food) and yes, I'll look over and explain your lease agreement (a lawyer daddy should be good for something!).

33. WHAT HAVE YOU LEARNED FROM YOUR CHILDREN?

While I haven't done the research, it seems that most of the "raising children" books focus on what parents should be teaching children and what they must learn from us. The material is adult-centered and written from an adult perspective. While it's true that parents do have a lot to offer their children, and should be teaching them the many lessons necessary to equip them for life as a responsible adult, I wonder whether the focus is in balance. Aren't there a lot of lessons we, as adults, should be learning from our children? If we learned these lessons, wouldn't the world be a better place and wouldn't we be better parents?

Children are humans in their purest form. Their spirits are free. They express their joy and curiosity for life and all of its riches. If you have any doubt, stop by a pre-school and watch the little kids on the playground. They laugh with joyful abandon. They create games and play together. They generally cooperate, play well together and work out their differences. They are quick to "make up" and quick to forget. They use positive words and seldom "get personal." Typically, they "keep hands, feet and all objects to self."

I want to learn more from my children. I want my spirit to be more like theirs. I want to laugh more and make life a playful adventure. I want more of life's activities to be turned into "silly" games. I want to spend more time thinking of more ways to have more fun. I want to laugh when things go wrong and I want to forget quickly. I want to live life in the moment, intently focused on the joys of the journey. I want to look forward and not back. I want to believe the best days of my life have not yet been lived. Then I want to wake up tomorrow and make that fortune come true. Just like a kid.

I hope you'll pause and take a moment to think about what you can learn from children and how your life would be better if you did. I hope you'll take the lessons our children have to teach us and apply them to your life. I'm confident you'll be a better parent and a better person. I'm confident being "childlike" can be a virtue!

PART IV:
WORDS YOU'LL NEED FOR THE JOURNEY

34. FAITH

The first word you'll need for your journey is faith. My faith in God is strong, resolute and unshakable. I've endured tough and lonely times, but I've never been alone. I've felt the heartache of love lost, but have never felt unloved. I've looked at the mountain of life from the bottom when the view was shrouded, the task seemingly impossible. Then I've awakened and realized that with God all things are possible. I was childless through my thirties, but somehow believed God would provide me with children in His own time. I've surrendered my life to Him and I've discovered a depth of peace and love unimaginable. I try to give Him thanks for my many blessings and rely on His Strength during the tough times. I can't do it on my own. My prayer each day is a simple one I've made up. "Dear God, give me the strength and wisdom to act in your light and love." I'm sure you've made up your prayer and you have your own stories of faith tested and faith applied.

I've always had my faith and have always felt God's guiding hand on my shoulder. However, I spent many years without understanding and truly believing. I thought I was in charge and in control. I felt bad, and took it personally, when things went wrong. I thought I was responsible for the feelings/misgivings/pain of others. I thought I had to carry my burdens alone. Those burdens were beyond me and wore me down. My life was not reaching it's spiritual potential and the burdens too heavy. I could go on, but you know the story from your own life.

For some, it might be difficult to comprehend why faith is important and how different your life will be with it. Imagine you are a sleek, white sailboat. The whiteness is startling to behold and obviously represents the inherent purity of your soul. Your sailboat is sturdy and buoyant, made to withstand the rough seas of life. It has no engine, but relies only on the God-supplied winds to travel on life's journeys. The problem is Earth consists of endless seas with powerful currents. One moment your boat is heading East in calm waters, and then the winds shift and storms engulf you. Oh my. What will you do?

In my imagery, your faith guides your sailboat to the most beautiful cove (probably a computer screen saver picture of Bora Bora!). But it's not enough to just be in the cove. There's more. You must be tethered to the ocean floor. Your faith in God connects you to Him. If you live in faith, you'll float and move (representing free will), but never stray too far (living true to God's Word). Without fully comprehending, you know you're anchored and made secure by God. What if you don't have faith? Your boat won't be tied down and will blow with the winds. It will be subject to every force, be constantly blown out to sea and tossed around by the vast forces of nature. You'll live a life exhausted at the burdens, responsibilities and uncertainties. You'll have the feeling of being constantly "blown off course." During these times, you'll feel frightened and alone with no one to turn to.

Even with faith embraced, we're a culture in search of knowledge outside of God's realm. I believe our search for "external" help is misplaced. What if you're turning outward, instead of inward, and looking for help in the wrong places? What if God has already given you everything you need? What if you're already equipped for the journey? What if, much like a parent packing a child's backpack, God has packed yours? What if every answer, every need, is already there for you? What if it's all there if only you'd ask? Get started and embrace your faith with passion. Spend your life basking in the warmth, glory and grace of God's love.

35. GRATITUDE

Imagine living a life filled with gratitude. What would that look like? Your first thought in the morning would be to give thanks for the new day. You'd be humbled at the sunrise and sound of birds chirping. No matter the struggles or difficulties, you'd be thankful for the blessings in your life. You'd spend a little extra time giving thanks for the blessings, because there are many. You have a roof over your head and food on the table. You have your family and your friends. Your ego would be small. Your sense of grace and gratitude for all you've been given and for this moment in time would be large and overwhelming. Your heart and spirit would be large as well, exuding a loving confidence. The people you meet would be lucky to cross your path because you'd say "Hi" and greet them with a smile. While facing the inevitable challenges of the day, you'd stay true to your core beliefs and not be swayed by the emotions of the moment. No one could do anything to you, because you wouldn't allow it. You'd see things clearly as they are and not as you want them to be. You'd have no sense of entitlement, because you're grateful for what you have. You wouldn't pursue objects or be jealous, because you're content with who you are and what you have. Over time, you'd want less, not more. You'd contribute anonymously to charity because of your need to give, not their need to receive. You'd give freely to others "because they need it more than you do."

What does a life of gratitude look like to you? Can you imagine living your life with a "gratitude-first" heart? Such a life would provide daily riches and rewards beyond your dreams. Live life "in gratitude."

36. COURAGE

If life were easy, we'd automatically make all the right choices. Our decisions, and the consequences that inevitably follow, would fall perfectly in place. The road would be smooth and our future would be predictably wonderful. However, experience tells us life doesn't work that way. We're faced with choices and decisions that are both unclear and difficult. Although we have a "true north" gut instinct to help guide us, we don't often follow it. Why? Because following your gut requires you to do things you don't want to do or face facts you don't want to face. Following your gut requires you to take the long, painful road and delay instant gratification. Making tough decisions requires you to do what you don't want to do, at a time when you don't want to do it. It's like driving through the fast food window and ordering vegetables and vitamin water. These good decisions often require that you don't follow the crowd. You may even lose friends in the process. When your so-called friends are waiving you down the wrong path, you must waive "goodbye" and take the other, lonely, fork in the road.

Making good decisions and following your gut requires something that's in short supply. Courage. Yes, it takes courage to walk away and choose the lonely path of a great life. It takes courage to say "no" to your so-called friends. It takes courage to say "no" to a relationship that's not good for you. It takes courage to seek help and overcome your own problems. It takes courage to change. It takes courage to lead an authentic life with an authentic voice. It takes courage to tell your kids "I don't care what your friends have or what their parents let them do. Our family has our own set of rules and our own unique way of doing things and we're not going to change just because someone else is doing it." It takes courage to give your children loving discipline, instead of being a "friend" who says, "yes" all the time.

I hope you grab an extra helping of courage. It's free and available to anyone. I hope you call your true friends (there's only a few) and ask them for their help and support in order to gain more courage. I hope you lead an authentic life with an authentic voice built on courage.

37. FORGIVENESS

Of all the words, forgiveness may present the greatest challenge. It's something we need to both give and receive.

On the giving side, have you forgiven someone lately? If so, did you find it easy to forgive or was it difficult? Did you quickly forgive someone after the harmful event, or did it take a long time? While forgiving someone is good for them, it is far more important for you to do the forgiving. Why? Until you've forgiven someone who's hurt you, you'll remain locked in the emotional chains of the past. You'll remain an emotional prisoner and carry the memory with you everywhere. Simply, it's the last act you need to perform to "get over it, once and for all." Please, do yourself an enormous favor, and forgive someone. Forgiveness of others will free your spirit and allow you to move forward with your wonderful life. Forgive them because they deserve it? Not necessarily. Forgive them because you deserve it more.

On the asking side, for whatever reason, it's not easy to ask for forgiveness. The more we need to be forgiven, the harder it is to ask. Especially when we do something that hurts a loved one, it seems our ego is in the way. Our own weaknesses prevent us from doing the right thing and the best thing: asking for forgiveness. If you want to live a life of accountability and bring your loved ones closer, learn to say "I'm sorry" and "I apologize." Then follow those words with "Will you forgive me?" These words are especially powerful when you say them to your children. You are modeling an important behavior they need to learn and showing your children enormous respect. Watch their expressions and attitudes change and bring them closer.

If you're good at taking responsibility for your actions and apologizing, if you're good at asking for forgiveness, your friends and loved ones will be lucky indeed. If you're also quick to forgive others, your life will be truly blessed. What are you waiting for? There's someone in your life at this moment that you need to forgive. Forgive them because you deserve it more. Oh, and by the way, the person that needs forgiving may be you. So, give yourself the ultimate gift. Forgive yourself and you'll be rewarded with a truly extraordinary life filled with love and joy. Do it today!

PART V: CONCLUSION

My wish is that this is your fortune: You have not yet lived the best days of your life. Then, tomorrow, you wake up with a new attitude. You begin living a life of success based on four words. You have a small goal a day. Your heart is filled with love. Your "little voice" speaks words of self-love and compassion. Your first reaction is to laugh, especially when things go wrong. You live a life of accountability and you fully embrace the concept of being accountable. You don't work at a job and dread Mondays, but instead have discovered my Dad's secret. Like him, you "love what you do and have never worked a day in your life." You smile and inspire others. You have great friends and are a great friend in return. You have mentors you listen to. You've sought out others and are a great mentor. You have wisdom to share and pass on. In relationships, you've "loved and lost" and loved again. You're the treasure you want to find. If not already, you're in pursuit of a magnificent relationship with your best friend. You know what a healthy relationship looks like and you're working every day to be the spouse/mate/parent that God intended. You are living up to and into your potential. If you have children, they are lucky to have you as their parent. You understand "it's not about you," and you're trying to raise your child to be a respectful, responsible and independent adult. You give them age-appropriate choices and decisions, and they experience the natural consequences that follow. You tell them you love them unconditionally, in the same way God loves them. You don't give them what they want, but what they need. You apply loving, consistent discipline and then laugh at the memories. You try to make life a game with "ice cream for all" at the end. Finally, you're living life's journey with some words you've carefully packed. Your faith is rock-solid and unshakable. You live each day filled with the blessings of gratitude. Courage is free and you've scooped up a healthy dose. You've forgiven others for the pain of your past. Finally, you've given yourself the most remarkable gift by forgiving yourself for all your human mistakes and miscalculations.

Is that all? Not exactly. This book was not an event, but a journey. I've shared my stories and challenges and how I've handled them. I've identified the things I wish I knew and captured my lessons learned late. Now it's your turn. I'd like to hear your stories.

I'd like you to share the things you wish you knew and your lessons learned late. I invite you to log on to my website, WWW.THING-SIWISHIKNEW.COM, and share your thoughts. I've broken my life into small stories and specific lessons learned late. I'd like you to do the same. Then, I'd like to collect your lessons and write a second book titled "Things You Wish You Knew – A Compendium of Your Lessons Learned Late." I'm excited about writing a book about you and look forward to hearing from you. I know you have a lot of wisdom to share. We can become a community helping a community. Finally, I imagine a third book (necessary to complete the trilogy) tentatively titled "We Found It and Knew It All Along – The Lessons We Didn't Need to Learn!"

ENDNOTES

Part I

The quotes from my father, and others used, are commonly attributed to such notables as Confucius, Lao Tzu, Ben Franklin, Vince Lombardi, Mark Twain and Yogi Berra.

From the film Star Wars, Episode V - The Empire Strikes Back: 20th Century Fox, 1980

Connie Cone Sexton, "Meet Your Fitness Instructor – Oh, and She's 89," The Arizona Republic, Wednesday, June 4, 2008

Larry Bossidy and Ram Charan, Execution: The Discipline of Getting Things Done (New York: Crown Publishing Group 2002)

Harvey Mackay, We Got Fired!:... And It's the Best Thing That Ever Happened to Us (New York: Ballantine Books 2004)

Part II

Keith Ablow, Living The Truth (New York: Little, Brown and Company 2007)

Terrence Real, How Can I Get Through to You? (New York: Simon & Schuster, Fireside 2002)

John M. Gottman and Nan Silver, The Seven Principles for Making Marriage Work (New York: Three Rivers Press 1999)

Gary Smalley, I Promise (Nashville: Integrity Publishers 2006)

Nancy Reagan, I Love You, Ronnie: The Letters of Ronald Reagan to Nancy Reagan (New York: Random House 2002)

Don Miguel Ruiz, The Mastery of Love (San Rafael: Amber-Allen Publishing 1999)

Gary Chapman, The Five Love Languages (Chicago: Northfield Publishing 2004)

Kevin Leman, The Birth Order Book (Grand Rapids: Revell 1998)

David Daniels and Virginia Price, The Essential Enneagram (San Francisco: HarperSanFrancisco 2000)

Part III

Mary Sheedy Kurcinka, Raising Your Spirited Child: A Guide for Parents Whose Child is More Intense, Sensitive, Perceptive, Persistent, Energetic (New York: HarperCollins 1991)

Kevin Leman, Making Children Mind Without Losing Yours (Grand Rapids: Revell 1984)

ACKNOWLEDGEMENTS

The material in this book took a lifetime to accumulate. None of it would have been possible to learn, even late, on my own. Thanks to my assistant of many years, Sherry Ledington, who was the first to urge me to "Write that book." To my sister Sharon, who encouraged me with the words "You are smarter than a two-year-old!" To my mentors, Frank Solich, Wally McNaught, David Ludtke, Hon. Irene F. Scott, Stef Tucker, Milt Hyman, David Weiss, Charlie Pulaski, and Rick Carlson, who believed in me when I didn't believe in myself. To my friends, Scott Bloom, Paul and Carol Wolff, Adrian Fiala, David Elrod, Howard Abrams, Lou Weller, Jeff DeBoer, Steve Renna, Dan Tucker and Charlie Siddle, who know the truth about me and like me anyway. To my English teacher, Stephanie Lonnquist, who refused to give me an "A" for my "B" quality papers. To my many professional friends and colleagues at my accounting firm, in my tax discussion group and at the ABA Tax Section, who've made me a vastly better lawyer and laughed at my song titles. To my golf buddies, Mike LaBauve and Steve Heller, who've helped me more with life, than with my golf game! To my friends at The Wharton School of Business, especially Kathy Pearson and David Wessels, who've taught me there are new ways to think about business and life.

The sections of the book on relationships and raising children were inspired by the teachings of Pastor Kelly Bender and staff at Paradise Valley United Methodist Church, as well as the youth program led by Andrea Andress and the pre-school program led by Mindy Sobraske. I can't thank you enough for your kindness and spiritual guidance. Thanks also to my PVUMC "home improvement" friends, especially Gwen and Doug Parker who've taught me about giving to the least among us.

ABOUT THE AUTHOR

Fred is a certified specialist in tax law, certified by the State Bar of Arizona. He works with a national accounting firm in Phoenix. In 2007, the International Who's Who of Business Lawyers named him to Who's Who Legal. In 2008, he was named an outstanding alumnus in the field of law by Lincoln Southeast High School and recognized as a Master by the University of Nebraska Lincoln. Fred was featured in an article on golf fitness in <u>The New York Times</u> and has appeared in an infomercial with Mike LaBauve on <u>The Golf Channel</u>. He is a divorced dad with three amazing gifts, Aaron (13), Tyler (11) and Olivia (7).

Made in the USA
Las Vegas, NV
30 May 2022

49550608R00111